809. 9113

A Teacher's Introduction to Postmodernism

A Teacher's Introduction to Postmodernism

Ray Linn
Cleveland Humanities High School
Reseda, California

NCTE Teacher's
Introduction Series

National Council of Teachers of English
1111 W. Kenyon Road, Urbana, Illinois 61801-1096

Manuscript Editors: Robert A. Heister, David A. Hamburg
Humanities & Sciences Associates

Production Editors: Michael Greer, Jamie Hutchinson

Interior Design: Tom Kovacs for TGK Design

Cover Design: Barbara Yale-Read

NCTE Stock Number: 50098-3050

It is the policy of NCTE in its journals and other publications to provide a forum for the open discussion of ideas concerning the content and the teaching of English and the language arts. Publicity accorded to any particular point of view does not imply endorsement by the Executive Committee, the Board of Directors, or the membership at large, except in announcements of policy, where such endorsement is clearly specified.

Library of Congress Cataloging-in-Publication Data

Linn, Ray.
  A teacher's introduction to postmodernism / Ray Linn.
      p. c.m. — (NCTE teacher's introduction series, ISSN 1059-0331; 5)
  Includes bibliographical references and index.
      1. Postmodernism. 2. Postmodernism (Literature) 3. Postmodernism and education. 4. Multiculturalism. I. Title. II. Series.
  B831.2.L56 1996
  149—dc20   96-15312
                                                                                    CIP

For my students
at Jordan and Cleveland High Schools

Contents

Foreword

A Teacher's Introduction to Postmodernism is the fifth in a series of books that are especially useful to teachers of English and language arts at all levels. Ours is a wide-ranging discipline, and important scholarly developments in various aspects of our field can be highly complex, not to mention voluminous. We often wish we had the time to take courses or do extended personal reading in topics such as deconstruction, psycholinguistics, rhetorical theory, and the like. Realistically, each of us can read intensively and extensively only in those areas that are of special interest to us or that are most closely related to our work. The Teacher's Introduction series, then, is geared toward the intellectually curious teacher who would like to get an initial, lucid glance into rich areas of scholarship in our discipline.

Let me stress three things that are *not* intended in *A Teacher's Introduction to Postmodernism* and in other books in this series. First, the books are in no way shortcuts to in-depth knowledge of any field. Rather, these straightforward treatments are intended to provide introductions to major ideas in the field and to whet the appetite for further reading. Second, the books do not aim to "dumb down" complicated ideas, sanitizing them for an imagined "average reader." Many of the ideas are quite challenging, and we don't want to send the message that every subject which is important to English and language arts teachers should be taught directly in the classroom. The personal enrichment of the teacher is paramount here. A great deal of misery might have been avoided in the 1960s if teachers had been doubly urged to learn about grammars new and old—that's part of being a well-rounded teacher—but to *avoid* bringing their new insights, tree diagrams and all, directly into the classroom.

We are grateful to Ray Linn for taking on the formidable work of writing so lucidly about the complexities of postmodernism. We welcome your comments on the *Teacher's Introduction* concept.

Charles Suhor
Deputy Executive Director, NCTE

Acknowledgments

Not all high school teachers have been lucky enough to be around students and teachers who are willing to enter the world of abstract thought, but I have, and I want to thank them for the many class discussions and conversations which have kept my teaching life interesting, and which eventually led to this book. On students, I've always felt that the reason they exist is to help their teachers through complicated books and ideas, and in serving this purpose mine have been especially patient and helpful—far more than they realize. So have other teachers I've been around, and here I especially want to thank Paul Paye, Bob Norris, Larry Kupers, Marty Kravchak, Jeremy Elkins, John Hartzog, Richard Coleman, Neil Anstead, and a twelfth-grade interdisciplinary team of humanities teachers that includes Melanie Miller, Chris Biron, Donna Hill, Jerry DeBono, Howard Wilf, and Nina Gifford. I also want to thank the people who helped to get this manuscript into publishable form, especially our school secretary Jody Stanfield, Cindy Dale of the Armand Hammer Museum at UCLA, Timothy Crusius (whose encouragement and criticism of an early draft were especially helpful), Marlo Welshons and Michael Greer at NCTE, and Robert Heister of Humanities & Sciences Associates. Above all, I want to thank Nina and Neil—without Nina, who spent endless hours questioning and editing the manuscript, it would never have been completed; and without my boss Neil, who lied and assured me that it could be finished "in a couple of weeks," it would never have been started.

Introduction

This book grew out of an interdisciplinary humanities unit which a group of teachers have been developing during the last few years at Cleveland Humanities High School, an integration magnet in Los Angeles. Our twelfth-grade curriculum focuses on the history of the modern Western world, and we begin with the scientific and capitalist revolutions, Brunelleschi's discovery of perspective, Shakespeare's Renaissance plays, and Descartes's epistemological turn. We trace this history down to the present day, focusing on several major cultural developments in the modern period, e.g., the Enlightenment, romanticism, existentialism, and the development of mass-produced, technological societies in the twentieth century. At the end of the year we try to present some "radical alternatives" to what we see as the prevailing Western traditions, alternatives which have included Buddhism, Tolstoy's Christianity, and A. S. Neill's *Summerhill* approach to child rearing. Then, a few years ago, we read that a "strange specter is roaming through Europe: the Postmodern" (Docherty 1993, 1), and so we decided to end the year with a new unit on postmodernism.

In working out our unit, we came to several conclusions which help to explain the way this book is written. First, postmodernism is best regarded as a widespread cultural development which has been taking shape during the last few decades and which is important because of its treatment of several interrelated themes; especially significant are the following:

- truth;
- language and its relation to thought and to the world;
- reason, science, and technology;
- human nature and the self;
- the Other (an individual or group considered as different);
- power and oppression; and
- creativity and the aesthetic.

Second, we think that postmodern thought makes sense only in contrast to an earlier Western cultural development which began to take shape during the seventeenth and eighteenth centuries and which continues to influence us today, a way of thinking about our situation in the world which can be called "modernism." Chapters 1, 3, and 4 are organized with this contrast in mind, and thus they focus on the shift from a modernist to a postmodernist perspective in philosophy, literature, history, and art.

Finally, we concluded that if ever a humanities topic required interdisciplinary treatment, it is postmodernism, and thus the interdisciplinary approach of this book. In our opinion, English teachers who stick too closely to their discipline miss the significance of postmodernism. For example, in order to understand why postmoderns are attacking the Western faith in reason, it is not enough to focus on the Age of Reason literature which most of our English teachers hate to teach. We must also look at the rational architectural boxes built in the International Style, at the social and ecological consequences of trying to force the world into a more "rational" order, and at philosophical developments from Nietzsche to Wittgenstein and Rorty. Nor can teachers understand the postmodern "language is everything" theme without focusing on twentieth-century social and anthropological theory. This is why there is a chapter on social theory, specifically, on "Human Nature, Evolution, and a History of the Modern World."

Some readers have suggested that the most important question raised by this book is whether a unit on postmodernism can be justified. Does a postmodern view of our situation in the world have much value in a democratic, capitalist, and multicultural society? More than a few critics tend to dismiss postmodernism as an elitist school of thought brought to America by a group of French nihilists, and these critics see it as having little relevance to serious social and political problems that need more than postmodern "deconstruction." In our opinion the critics are wrong, and one of the reasons Richard Rorty is at the center of our story is that his pragmatic approach helps us to see why postmodernism is more useful to us today than the modernism it seeks to replace. In the final chapter, "Postmodernism and Multiculturalism," we discuss how a postmodern perspective on the world might influence teaching in a positive way.

The issue of the value of studying postmodernism is obviously a matter of opinion, but it is hard to deny that postmodernism forces students to reflect on fundamental questions about our situation in the world, questions about who we are, how we got this way, and what we should do. For some examples: Is anthropologist Clifford Geertz right when he says that human beings are "incomplete animals" (1973, 46) who lack an essential nature that causes us to think and feel as we do— so that all of our thoughts and feelings are "manufactured" (50) by the culture that we grow up in? And are Foucault and Lyotard right in suggesting that human beings are always driven by a will to power, and that reason, instead of liberating us, is simply another tool for dominating the Other? Should we also accept Rorty's claim that we have no reason to take the concept of truth seriously? Finally, is Rorty right when he tells English teachers to forget their worries about whether a sentence accurately represents the world and to simply focus on whether their vocabulary will "get us what we want" (1982, 150)? We've had few students who could remain indifferent to such questions.

But perhaps the most interesting questions raised by postmodern thought are a result of its foregrounding of language and making it the center of everything human. Comments such as Rorty's, that human beings are merely "centerless webs" (1989, 88) of "incarnated vocabularies" (80) and Heidegger's, that "language speaks" man (1971, 215–16) rather than the reverse, and Wittgenstein's, that a human being is like a "fly [trapped in the] fly-bottle" (1958, 103) of language, and Derrida's, that "there is nothing outside the text" (1976, 158), are hard to sleep through. So is the "death of the author" debate—i.e., the debate about whether English teachers should try to get behind an author's words to some kind of original thought or intention that the author was trying to "express," or whether they should follow Barthes, who says that when Shakespeare wrote *Hamlet*, there was nothing in his head but a "ready-formed dictionary" (1992, 117).

Perhaps above all, the postmodern challenge presents us with the question of whether we should change our self-image. First, should we continue to think of ourselves as governed by an essential nature, or should we go postmodern and see ourselves as lacking an essential nature and as governed by a particular human language? And second, should we continue to accept the modernist view that we can discover truth in the world and therefore strive to base our lives on its foundation? Or should we go postmodern and see ourselves as linguistic dreamers who find nothing, but who are able to create the worlds we live in? The issue is whether we should tell our students that what is most important in human life is our imaginative language—not only because it creates worlds, but also because it sometimes creates beautiful worlds.

Here it should be emphasized that in discussing various thinkers and artists under the headings of "modernism" and "postmodernism," this book inevitably plays down their uniqueness. Nor is it the complete

story of postmodernism, but rather is designed solely as a brief introduction for the general reader, with few technical terms (which is why
we have not included a glossary). The book is also highly selective—
Why so much on Rorty and so little on Heidegger and Derrida? Why
two novels by Jerzy Kosinski and none by Salman Rushdie? One reason
is that we wanted to present only works and authors which we have
taught in an integrated American classroom with students new to the
subject. A great deal of important postmodern writing is too difficult to
use at an introductory level, and thus it is not discussed here. Some of
what has been omitted, on Derrida and the hermeneutic tradition, is
covered in two other books in the Teacher's Introduction Series, *A
Teacher's Introduction to Deconstruction*, by Sharon Crowley, and *A Teacher's
Introduction to Philosophical Hermeneutics*, by Timothy Crusius.

1 From Modern to Postmodern Western Philosophy

Toward the end of his last play, written just before the beginning of the modernist era, the West's greatest poet asked those of the next generation to think of their lives in the following way:

> You do look, my son, in a movèd sort,
> As if you were dismayed. Be cheerful, sir.
> Our revels now are ended. These our actors,
> As I foretold you, were all spirits, and
> Are melted into air, into thin air.
> And, like the baseless fabric of this vision,
> The cloud-capped towers, the gorgeous palaces,
> The solemn temples, the great globe itself—
> Yea, all which it inherit—shall dissolve
> And, like this insubstantial pageant faded,
> Leave not a rack behind. We are such stuff
> As dreams are made on, and our little life
> Is rounded with a sleep.
>
> —*The Tempest* (4.1.165–77)

Shakespeare's advice was rejected, and thus began the modernist culture which has continued to dominate Western thought for several centuries.

Today, however, the postmoderns are arguing that it is time to move beyond modernist culture, and thus there is an interesting fight going on. To understand some of the issues in the fight, we will begin this chapter with a look at the origins of modernism in Western philosophy, beginning with brief discussions of Descartes, Locke, the philosophes, and Kant. We will then turn to some of the criticisms of early modern philosophy, first by Hume in the eighteenth century, then by the romantics, Darwin, and Nietzsche in the nineteenth century, and finally by Saussure and Wittgenstein in the first part of the twentieth century. In discussing Nietzsche, Saussure, and Wittgenstein, we will also see the basis for a distinctively postmodern view of things—the kind of view which is expressed by Roland Barthes, Jacques Derrida, and Richard Rorty. It should be emphasized that in discussing these key figures, the goal isn't to give a complete account of the transition from modern to postmodern thought, but only to give a brief intellectual history while highlighting some of the major issues in today's debate.

As we will try to show, to a large extent the debate is over two different ways of thinking about language and the role it plays in human life. But as was mentioned in the introduction, the larger issue is over how we should view ourselves. At the start of the story, Descartes tells us that we are unique creatures who are endowed with a rational nature, and he also tells us that we should strive to be true to this nature. For Descartes, as for the modernists who followed him, this involves striving for "knowledge," which is thought of as an accurate and certain representation of nature, a representation which will provide a solid foundation for human life.

At the end of our story Rorty will be telling us that such knowledge cannot be located, that there will be no foundations, and that we have no "essential nature" to be true to. For Rorty, we human beings are unique, but only because of a linguistic ability that enables us to create worlds through "redescriptions." Since these redescriptions are based on nothing more than our imaginative ability with words, there will never be anything "solid" about them. In other words, Rorty wants us to drop Descartes's modernist project and to finally accept Shakespeare's vision of human beings as "actors" living in an "insubstantial pageant" founded on nothing but a "baseless . . . vision." But before discussing Rorty's postmodernism, we need to look more closely at Descartes and the tradition which could not accept that human life is "such stuff as dreams are made on."

Descartes and the Search for Foundations

Perhaps Descartes's philosophy and modernism in general should be seen as a secular crusade that began to emerge in the seventeenth century, stimulated especially by the scientific revolution. It was also partially a reaction to medieval crusades that fostered ignorance, intolerance, and terrible religious wars, and perhaps to the chronic unavailability of God. In philosophy the origins of the new crusade are first clearly visible in the writings of Descartes, and his "I think, therefore I am" can be seen as marking the beginning of an early modern manifesto.

In developing his philosophy Descartes apparently felt an intense need for certainty, and as a result he initiated a major shift in Western philosophy. It was a shift away from the traditional philosophical preoccupation with wisdom to a new preoccupation with acquiring "knowledge." The new idea was that first we must talk about what is certain, and only then will we have sufficient grounds for talking about what is real and how we should live. Questions about reality and morality are still significant, but they are not as important as finding a solid foundation for human life.

While searching for a foundation, Descartes decided that a new method was needed for acquiring knowledge, and this method dominated Western philosophy throughout the modernist period and into the twentieth century. It is discussed in the second part of *Discourse on Method* (see *The Essential Descartes,* 113–21), and it is usually called "the method of systematic doubt." If you use it you will need to survey all of your general beliefs about the world and try to find reasons for doubting them; then, if there is even the slightest reason to doubt a belief, you must discard it. For example, you might at first believe that the desk in front of you is beige in color, but if you use Descartes's method, you will realize that it only *appears* beige in this particular light, and only to animals with color vision. In the dark, or to a color-blind dog, it looks different. So is it really beige? Since you have no reason to prefer one appearance over another, the belief that the desk is beige becomes doubtful and must therefore be discarded. If you keep using this method you can easily reach the same conclusion that modernist Bertrand Russell reached more than three hundred years after Descartes in *Problems of Philosophy* (1959, 7–12): that all ideas about the desk's properties can also be doubted. It should be stressed that the goal of all this doubting was to find ideas which could not be reasonably doubted, for only such ideas, like the axioms of geometry, could provide the foundation for a secure theory of knowledge.

When Descartes used his method of doubt he first came to the conclusion that *all* of his ideas about the external world were doubtful. Descartes argued that this conclusion follows from the possibility of dreaming. So ask yourself: How do you know that you are not now dreaming? Is it not possible that you failed to wake up this morning, and that you are now dreaming that you are reading a book? Some dreams are quite realistic, and there doesn't seem to be any test that proves you are not now dreaming. Tests like slapping yourself or asking a person next to you if you're awake prove nothing because you could be dreaming that you are performing such tests. In other words, the distinction between a dream experience and an awake experience is not based on reason. And if you cannot prove that you are not now dreaming, then you cannot prove any of your beliefs about the external word, for they could all be part of your dream.

But because of Descartes's hunger for a certain foundation—postmoderns will later call it a "hang-up"—he did not give up, and he finally arrived at an idea that he thought was certain: that he existed.

For regardless of whether he was sleeping or awake, he was undeniably doubting, and for there to be doubt there had to be something—a self—which was doubting. There just could not be any kind of mental activity unless there was an individual mind that was thinking, and so the thinker must exist. As Descartes said: "I think, therefore I am," and with this line he thought he had arrived at a solid foundation for a theory of knowledge.

After concluding that he was a mental self that thinks (only the thinking mind is certain—the body could be part of the dream), Descartes next focused on one of his most important ideas, the idea of God; and after much reasoning he concluded that God must exist too. Furthermore, Descartes reasoned that, since God is good, He wouldn't want to deceive His children, which in turn led Descartes to the conclusion that he could, after all, be certain of clear and distinct ideas about the external world. Most modernists after Descartes found the God argument deeply flawed, and without God as backup the foundationalist project became much more difficult. But because knowledge seemed so important, especially with the decline of traditional religion, Western philosophers kept struggling for centuries.

There are several reasons why Descartes's philosophy is important to the modern story. First, he made the search for foundations all-important; more specifically, he told Westerners that they must start their intellectual lives with the search for representations of the world which are absolutely certain. Second, he discouraged Westerners from relying on God, Divine Revelation, or the priests. Although not an atheist, Descartes no longer had faith in the medieval crusade based on the Word of God and the Church. Nor did he place his faith in the traditions of his ancestors, which were just too full of ignorance, error, and uncertainty to be relied upon for a secure foundation in life. Nor did he expect anything positive to come from human feeling—from "animal passion" that prevents clear thought and always messes up everything. Finally, he could see nothing positive coming from our linguistic imagination: What kind of solid foundation could be provided by some artist's dream life?

Rejecting all of these traditional guides to human life, Descartes replaced them with a single Savior, which the Greeks called "Reason." By this word Descartes meant more than reaching conclusions based on premises or bits of evidence; what he meant was inquiry based on the human faculty of grasping necessary connections. This is the God-given faculty that is used in discovering the undoubtable truths of mathematics, and it, rather than the Church, is what led Descartes to God. It is also the faculty that we should rely on always.

Descartes's human being is thus a special kind of creature in the universe. He is special because he has a rational essence, and because of his essence, he is fundamentally detached from his surroundings. As a detached, rational agent, he is free to choose what to believe and how to act, and if he chooses to be true to his rational essence, he will be able to accomplish two things: first, he will be able to defeat the unruly passions that lead to error and an immoral life; second, he will be able to discover the truth about the rational universe which surrounds him. Here it should be noted that for all of his doubting, Descartes never seemed to seriously doubt Galileo's famous claim that "the book of nature is written in the language of mathematics." If this were not the case, if there were no rational order to be discovered, the claim that reason gives us the truth about nature would seem doubtful.

Locke and the Search for Empirical Foundations

Later in the seventeenth century, a fight started between the strict followers of Descartes, the "rationalists" who believed that they should stick to reason alone, and the more lax "empiricists" who followed Bacon, Hobbes, and Locke. The empiricists were also hungry for foundations, and in writing his famous *An Essay Concerning Human Understanding*, Locke tells us ". . . my purpose . . . is to inquire into the original, certainty, and extent of human knowledge; together, with the grounds and degrees of belief, opinion, and assent . . ." (1959, 7). But Locke and the empiricists formed a less strict group of modernists because they felt that reason must be supplemented with experience if it is to provide us with knowledge and a much needed foundation. It was this empiricist belief that in making a knowledge claim we should not ignore experience, which the rationalists rejected, and the rationalist belief that some ideas are in the mind at birth, which the empiricists rejected, that led to the fight.

From the postmodern point of view, it is easy to overemphasize this fight, for both sides agreed on several modernist beliefs: that the search for knowledge and foundations is extremely important in human life; that an essential nature, rather than language or culture, gives determinate shape to the way we think and live in the world; that there is no special moral problem about the Other; and finally, that reason is the best guide in human life, and not tradition, religion, or the imagination. Although *An Essay Concerning Human Understanding* is an empiricist treatise, Locke insists that human beings must always follow reason. The most important of the empiricists, David Hume, later made this idea look absurd, but we will discuss Hume at the end of this section on modernism.

The Philosophes and the Social Gospel of Modernism

Against an eighteenth-century background of increasing scientific and economic success, a group of French radicals, the philosophes, turned early modernism into a major secular crusade. In particular they encouraged Westerners to turn against established traditions, like the monarchy and the Church, and instead to bring about a more humane future through reason and science. Beginning with his *Letters on England*, Voltaire praises Newton's science and Locke's empiricism, and he singles out Locke for having demonstrated that we are rational beings for whom knowledge is the key to happiness.

A few years later, in their highly influential *Encyclopédie* articles, the enlightened philosophes consistently contrasted an ignorant religious tradition to a rational science, and they left no doubt that it was science which would lead human beings to the Promised Land. With the continued discovery of scientific truth, humankind would overcome ignorance, poverty, and oppression and move into a more glorious age. While not everyone went as far as Condorcet, who promised that even death would be left behind (Jones 1969, 3), there was a consensus that a devotion to reason and science made progress inevitable. While not systematic philosophers, the philosophes played a major role in popularizing the modernist view of the world, and as much as anyone else they turned reason into a religion.

Kant's Elaborate Version of Modernism

Writing toward the end of the eighteenth century, Immanuel Kant presented a strong case for modernism. Devoted to truth and secure rational foundations, he spent his life working out the most elaborate rational theories in human history. Specifically, in *Critique of Pure Reason*, he developed a theory of knowledge; in *Critique of Practical Reason* and *Fundamental Principles of the Metaphysic of Morals*, a theory of what is morally good; and in *Critique of Judgement*, theories of beauty and the sublime. If ever there was a high priest of reason, it was surely Kant, and for many living in a postmodern era, his devotion to reason is almost inconceivable.

With regard to Kant's ideas about a moral life, he agreed with Descartes that reason alone is what is important, and that tradition, God, feeling, and the imagination are irrelevant to moral decisions. Kant even argued that "the moral worth of an action does not lie in the effect expected from it" (1987b, 26); and thus your moral decisions should not be influenced by considerations of consequences like pleasure or pain, life or death. What alone makes an act like telling the truth good, and what alone should guide a moral decision, is the principle or rule which will be followed by choosing to act in that way.

In Kant's language, in acting morally you will "act only on that maxim whereby thou canst at the same time will that it become a universal law" (1987b, 49). This moral principle, which Kant calls "the categorical imperative," asserts that when you choose to act according to a rule which should be universal, you are acting morally, regardless of the consequences of your action. For example, if you are in a situation in which you must decide whether it would be permissible to lie instead of telling the truth, ask yourself whether all human beings should lie whenever it is convenient. If the answer is no, then you have a rational duty to tell the truth. Since only rational animals can conceive of and act according to universal rules, only when we choose to act according to such rules are we true to our essential rational nature.

In "On a Supposed Right to Lie from Altruistic Motives" (Rachels 1986, 140), Kant acknowledged that in some situations, telling the truth might lead to a friend's death while a lie would save her life; but even in this case Kant insists that considerations of the specific consequences must be ignored. Feeling must also be ignored, and Kant insists that if you were to help a friend only out of pity, your act would not be a moral act. If, on the other hand, your decision to help follows only from a consideration of the universal principle that rational animals should always help other rational animals, then you are doing your rational duty and acting morally.

In response to the more recent charge that there is something cold-hearted about this strictly rational approach to morality, an enlightened Kant might have replied that feelings have not improved human life and that in the eighteenth century everybody could see that moral progress was tied to reason and science, not animal feeling. A critical postmodern might also point out that there is something rigid and unimaginative about a life devoted to the mechanical application of universal rules. But how could the imagination provide any kind of solid foundation for human life—how could it produce anything more than a baseless "insubstantial pageant"?

In *Critique of Judgement,* his last major work on aesthetic theory, Kant lightens up a little and does bring in the importance of the imagination. He specifically argues that for a natural object or artwork to be experienced as "beautiful," it must please the imagination rather than simply satisfy reason by conforming to rules. But he also insists that to be beautiful, a natural object or artwork must at the same time please our rational nature, that is, please the part of us which wants order, unity, and purpose. In Kant's words, to be beautiful an object must have a form that gives us a sense of "purposiveness" (Kemp 1968, 103) when we contemplate it in an impersonal, "disinterested" (Kant 1986, 49) way.

A beautiful object is thus an object like a rose, which has a form so perfectly designed that it gives us a sense that it must have been designed to please us as rational animals. Whether a beautiful rose or a play like Racine's *Phèdre*, perfectly designed objects are important because they reassure us that our rational attempts to understand the universe make sense, which would be the case if the universe were created by a rational designer. Because of our need to be reassured that our devotion to reason's progress makes sense, "barbaric" emotion (Kant 1986, 65) in an artwork must be held to a minimum; if emotion or sensuality are too strong, we are not able to focus on the rational form that alone satisfies our essential rational nature.

By bringing in the importance of the imagination in art, Kant freed artists from the oppressive neoclassical belief that they had to follow rules in making an artwork. And in stressing the importance of the imagination, he moves toward postmodernism. On the other hand, Kant did not free artists from the modernist idea that a work of art must be representational, for in order to give us a sense of a purposeful nature, a painting or play must also give us a sense that it represents nature.

It should also be noted that this idea of representation—that the artist must hold a mirror up to nature—means that the artist will try to give his society an image of the world that fits in with its commonsense beliefs, thus reassuring the society that it has reasoned its way to the right beliefs. But, as postmoderns point out, such art—art, in other words, that a society calls "realistic"—also reassures a society about its traditional prejudices rather than helping it transcend them.

But Kant saw things differently. He wanted an art which would reassure us of the value of reason not only because he believed that reason was the key to a moral life, but also because, in the *Critique of Pure Reason*, he had earlier demonstrated that reason is sadly limited when it comes to gaining knowledge about nature. Far more skeptical than Descartes, he argued that we can know some things about the world as it appears after it is organized by the human mind. But that is all, and we cannot know anything about what the world is like "in itself," independent of its appearance in the mind. Specifically, we cannot even know whether the external world is material or spiritual in nature. Nor can we know anything about the specific nature of a self that endures through time.

In sum, while Kant was continuing the modernist tradition, in his writings the foundation provided by human reason seems far more questionable. His view of the mind is also important to later doubts about the modernist project: before Kant it was easy to think of the mind as passively registering realistic pictures of the world, like a copy machine, but for Kant the mind becomes an active, organizing synthesizer of sense experience. In other words, it is creative and it "constructs" its picture of the world. Postmoderns will later agree on this point, but whereas Kant argues that the mind constructs its picture on the basis of its innate mental categories, postmoderns will argue that it constructs on the basis of an internalized public language. Finally, Kant argues that all human minds think in terms of the same basic innate categories, and thus all human beings are substantially alike. In other words, for Kant, culture and language are at the surface of human life, and underneath them human beings worldwide share the same shaping rational nature. If such an underlying substantial and shaping human nature did not exist, the modernist goal of trying to be true to our nature would seem incoherent.

Hume's Attack on the Modernist Program

In developing his theory of knowledge Kant was partially attempting to answer the Scottish empiricist David Hume, who wrote his main work, *A Treatise of Human Nature*, in 1739–1740. Hume is one of the great exceptions in the early modern era, and he is being discussed after Kant because he presents the first major attack on the modernist program. Since Hume is so important to all later evaluations of the modernist project, we need to examine him more closely than the thinkers discussed thus far.

Starting from the empiricist assumption that all ideas are derived from experience, Hume set out to show the great limits of reason and, perhaps more than any Western philosopher, he succeeded. Hume is most famous for showing that reason does not show us whether any of the following ideas are true: that there is a self which stays the same over time (Descartes's "I"); that there are necessary cause-and-effect relationships (say, between a flaming match and a burnt finger); that the natural regularities observed so far will continue in the future (such as the sun rising in the morning); that there exist either material or mental objects (atoms, God, individual minds); and finally, that any human act is morally right or wrong. In addition to demonstrating that these ideas are not based on reason, Hume also tries to show that it is our animal nature that gives rise to them. From a postmodern point of view, he is right about the first point, but what he says on the second needs to be supplemented.

With regard to the idea of a self—the idea that you are the same person today as yesterday—Hume shows that there is no evidence which supports it. Evidence gathered through introspection shows only changing impressions, passions, and ideas, and nothing permanent in addition to them. In Hume's language, introspection reveals only a "bundle" (1958, 252) of changing impressions and ideas, rather than a self that remains the same over time and unites these impressions and ideas. Is there a self, despite the lack of evidence? Maybe, but maybe not—what Hume shows is that there is no rational way of knowing.

Although this doubt about the existence of an unchanging self is also found earlier in the sixteenth-century *Essays* of Montaigne, Hume's empirical argument is much more forceful, and it points toward two postmodern claims: that we have no fixed, essential nature, and that whatever one's self-concept, it is not based on direct introspection. On the other hand, Hume argues unconvincingly that a sense of self is simply a consequence of certain private associations evoked when an individual reflects on her past. He never suggests that the belief might result from public practices and, in particular, from an internalized language.

Hume is also concerned with another commonsense idea which is essential in modern science—the idea that there are necessary cause-and-effect relationships between events. Again, after examining the evidence, he shows that there is no reason to accept this idea either. For example, if you watch me yank the desk out from under a sleeping student and then see him fall to the floor, you would only directly see a succession of contiguous events, one immediately following the other. You would first have experience of one event (the desk yanked out from under the sleeping student), then a second (the student hitting the floor). What Hume emphasizes is that you have not experienced the necessary connection between the two events; that is, you have not actually witnessed the first event *making* or *forcing* the occurrence of the second event. He acknowledges that you have also had the same experience repeatedly—first, the removal of support, then a falling object—but he also points out that this repetition does not add necessity or "must" to what you have actually experienced. Just because one of two contiguous events has repeatedly followed the other does not prove that it was caused by the first event (1958, 77).

It is thus possible that we live in a universe in which some events repeatedly follow others without being caused by them. Hume adds that there doesn't seem to be any a priori reason why an event in nature must have a cause. If you were to say, for example, that the universe must have a cause, and that cause was God, Hume would quickly ask you if God was caused. Is there an answer? Do events have causes? It is possible, but reason cannot decide.

Nor does it decide whether the same events will repeatedly follow others in the future (1958, 89). Since thus far the removal of an object's support has always been followed by the object's fall to the earth, we expect it to happen in the future. In other words, on the basis of such past "constant conjunctions," we tend to assume that nature is uniform, and all of our inductive reasoning from specific observations to general conclusions is based on this assumption. But how could we ever know whether the future will be like the past, since we haven't experienced the future? Why—based on what reason—should we believe that the constant repetition of one event following another will continue tomorrow? Nature has changed in the past, and it is logically possible that it will change tomorrow, so that the next time support is removed the student will rise to the ceiling. Again, Hume shows us that reason cannot provide us with the beliefs that are essential to survival.

To strengthen his case against reason, Hume tries to explain why, despite the lack of rational evidence, we nevertheless continue to believe that there are necessary cause-and-effect relations and also that the same relations we have observed in the past will continue into the future. Here he thinks that the key is psychological. Specifically, if two events are repeatedly connected in my experience, I will naturally associate the ideas of those two events, so that if I now become aware of the first event, the idea that it produces will lead me to *feel* that the second event *must* follow. For example, if *1* is repeatedly followed by *2* in my experience, when I next see a *1* I will inwardly expect that *2* must follow. Thus after *1212121213*, the *3* surprises. Here what is demonstrated is that the belief in a necessary causal connection is based on projection; as Stroud says, I "project" (1977, 86) my inner expectation or feeling of "must" onto the outside world. And it is this projection that leads me to say, "Of course he fell because I removed his support, and so will the next sinning student."

Hume's main point about causal relations is that the "must" or necessity which I think links two events together is not based on a sense impression that I get from the outside world; rather, it comes from within me as a result of the influence of the outside world on my animal nature. His other important point is that I have no reason to believe that the psychological feeling of necessity corresponds to an objective necessity between events in the external world. Fortunately, this lack of knowledge doesn't ruin my chances of survival since I cannot get rid of the animal nature which gives rise to my beliefs, and thus I will continue to act as though there were necessary connections in the world and that the next lion will be like the last. But the Savior is now my animal nature, and not reason.

Nor, argues Hume, can reason help us to discover what kinds of things exist in the external world. To determine whether God or matter exists, I would have to jump outside of my thoughts about the world and encounter it directly, as it exists independent of thought, but this is impossible. Thus, just as it is impossible to know if there are necessary causal relations outside of my thoughts, so it is impossible to know whether God or atoms are out there.

To conclude this discussion of the modernist search for what we can know, by 1739 it was becoming apparent that the answer is "nothing" and that Descartes's search for solid foundations was doomed. The interesting question is why, despite the lack of progress, Descartes's obsession continued to dominate intellectual life for such a long time, so that by the beginning of the twentieth century, Bertrand Russell could still begin his *Problems of Philosophy* with the same question: "Is there any knowledge which is so certain that no reasonable man could doubt it?" (1959, 7)—only to conclude once again that the answer is no. As the postmoderns say, it seems as though intellectuals could do something else with their time on earth.

In the *Treatise*, Hume also argues that reason alone does not lead to a moral life. For example, if you saw one human being murder another, you would normally conclude that something morally wrong had occurred, but Hume argues that this moral judgment was not based on observation or reason. Specifically, he claims that if you closely examine where your idea of "wrongness" came from, you will see that it did not come from what you actually observed while watching the murder. You did get an impression of an event—of the act of killing—but you did not get an impression of "wrongness" in addition to the event. Through reasoning, you can come up with a motive for the murder, and you can also come up with consequences which might follow, but reasoning alone will not add wrongness to these conclusions. For Hume, reasoning is what enables you to figure out how much money you've spent for dinner, and it helps you in calculating probabilities, but it cannot take you from "is" to "ought"—in this case, from the murder to the conclusion that it ought not to have happened. Hume even goes so far as to say,

"'Tis not contrary to reason to prefer the destruction of the whole world to the scratching of my finger!" (1958, 416).

In reaching such an extreme conclusion Hume relies primarily on the following argument: reason alone does not motivate action in the world; moral judgments do motivate action in the world; therefore, action based on moral judgments cannot be based on reason alone. The first premise of this argument is supported by Hume's account of action in general. As he puts it:

> Ask a man *why he uses exercise*; he will answer, *because he desires to keep his health*. If you then enquire, *why he desires health*, he will readily reply, because *sickness is painful*. If you push your enquiries farther, and desire a reason *why he hates pain*, it is impossible he can ever give any. This is an ultimate end, and is never referred to any other object.
>
> Perhaps to your second question, *why he desires health*, he may also reply, that *it is necessary for the exercise of his calling*. If you ask, *why he is anxious on that head*, he will answer, *because he desires to get money*. If you demand *Why? It is the instrument of pleasure*, says he. And beyond that it is an absurdity to ask for a reason. It is impossible there can be a progress *in infinitum;* and that one thing can always be a reason why another is desired. Something must be desirable on its own account, and because of its immediate accord or agreement with human sentiment and affection. (1962, 293)

Notice that in this passage, Hume is not denying that reasoning has an influence on our judgments and how we act in the world. As he says, if you want to avoid pain, reasoning can show you that you must stay healthy, and if you want health, it can show you that you must exercise; it can also show you that if you want pleasure, you must get money, and that if you want money, you must stay healthy. But why do you want to avoid pain, and why do you want pleasure? Here we come to something "desirable on its own account"—we come to "original ends" which spring from a nature we are born with, and not motives which are derived from reasoning. If something were not desirable on its own account, we would be indifferent to the conclusions of our reasoning, and thus we wouldn't act on them. For example, if we didn't already care about our health because of an original, unreasoned motive, the conclusion that we must exercise would not prompt action. Hume's point in this passage is thus that *reason alone* cannot prompt action, and, again, since moral judgments do prompt action, they cannot be based on reason alone. In other words, Descartes's and Kant's strictly national approach to morality is wrong.

How then should moral judgments be explained? Hume says that you will not find the answer until you "turn your reflection into your own breast" (1958, 469), and here again he emphasizes that because of our animal nature, the thoughts of certain events trigger certain feelings. For example, your moral judgment about one human being murdering another was simply an immediate response to a feeling that the idea of this event naturally produced within you—a feeling of disapproval that accompanied your idea of murder. This feeling of disapproval caused you to project "wrongness" onto the event, just as the feeling of necessity caused you to project necessary connections onto the world. Against Descartes and Kant, Hume's main point is that without feeling or passion there would be no moral behavior. Once again, reason alone leads nowhere.

In developing his moral theory, Hume insists that human beings are not total egoists and that we do have a disinterested concern for the well-being of others. Specifically, he claims that we approve of things that help others and also of things that give them pleasure, and we disapprove of things that are harmful to others or give them pain. In trying to explain this altruism, Hume emphasizes "sympathy" in the *Treatise* (1958, 316) and "benevolence" in his later *An Enquiry Concerning the Principles of Morals* (1962, 8–14). By "sympathy" he doesn't mean a specific feeling, but an innate inclination to share what we take to be the feelings of others, so that when the person next to me shows signs of joy, I will experience a similar good feeling, and when he cries, I will experience a similar feeling of sadness. Because of sympathy, not only are such passions "contagious," but I label "good" the personal qualities that help human beings or bring them pleasure (e.g., diligence, cheerfulness), and I disapprove of the qualities that bring them displeasure or do not help them (e.g., sullenness, laziness). In his *Enquiry*, Hume argues that it is a natural feeling of benevolence which provides the ultimate basis for disinterested moral judgments, and he defines benevolence as "whatever proceeds from a tender sympathy with others and a general concern for our kind and species" (1962, 10).

In sum, on the basis of his account of our ideas, actions, and moral values, in which all three are shown to have their ultimate roots in our passionate nature, Hume came to his shocking conclusion: "Reason is, and ought only to be, the slave of the passions, and can never pretend to any other office than to serve and obey them" (1958, 415). Such a line is obviously not that of a typical eighteenth-century modernist, and in radically separating reason from nature and also from the deep roots of a moral life, Hume moves toward postmodernism. It should also be noted that Hume's human being is no longer a detached rational essence, and without his active imagination, he would not be able to survive in the world.

Yet in many major ways Hume is a typical modernist. First, he continues to accept the modern belief that human life is given a determinate shape by an essential species nature, and he also suggests that we should be true to that nature. The beliefs and desires of Hume's human beings may no longer be governed by an essential rational nature, but they are still governed by an essential feeling nature.

Like other modernists who wrote before the rise of modern anthropology, Hume found it easy to think in terms of a very substantial nature which causes human beings everywhere to think and feel fairly much alike. Since our moral judgments come from our universal feeling nature, we tend to make the same moral judgments regardless of which society we grow up in. And although Hume lived during the modern slave era, he still assumed that human beings always regard murder as wrong, regardless of *who* gets murdered. The fact that the victim might be regarded as one of "them" rather than one of "us" is not thought of as a major fact in explaining our moral lives. Sympathy may be weaker for strangers, but that is no reason for thinking that the Other is a major moral problem.

Nor is there any reason to suppose that sympathy is manipulated by a public language, and at this point we come to the second characteristic that Hume shares with modernists: he has nothing to say about the role of language in shaping our specific beliefs. Ignorance can influence us, and so to some extent do social traditions, but not a public language. Here it is important to note a key modern assumption: that an individual's beliefs and desires are formed prior to the internalization of language and that language is merely a tool used to express thoughts that have already been formed. Given this assumption, plus that of a substantial essential nature, it is easy to accept Hume's empiricist belief that our ideas must be either innate or produced by direct bodily experience. Based on the same assumption, it was also easy for him to conclude that if it isn't reason, then innate feeling must be at the root of our moral lives.

This simple either/or—reason, or passion?—pervades early modern thought, and it continues to pervade the thought of the romantics who followed Hume's emphasis on feeling. Even in his discussion of "artificial" virtues (e.g., why I think it is wrong to take your property) (1958, 484), where Hume does take up the role of convention, he argues that in addition to convention, there is a natural sympathy for all human beings. After all, something deep in human nature must play a decisive role in determining how an individual comes to think and feel about the world. Even if the foundation isn't reason, the specific shape of our lives couldn't be determined by an insubstantial language that enters our heads. Shakespeare just couldn't be right in suggesting that our values are controlled by a "baseless . . . vision."

Three Nineteenth-Century Criticisms of Modernism

Despite Hume, during the first half of the nineteenth century the devotion to reason continued to dominate Western societies, as is most obviously seen in the rapid development of science and the increasingly rational approach to economic and industrial development. In early-nineteenth-century philosophy the same devotion is found in Hegel, whose *Philosophy of History* argues that history has a purpose in that it is the march of reason toward freedom and a better way of life, with human societies inevitably moving forward toward increasingly rational social institutions and moral codes. A few years later Karl Marx praised the emerging capitalist society for its introduction of a more rational system of production, and he also predicted that the trend toward greater rationality and freedom would continue with the transition to socialism.

But during the same period major intellectual developments were beginning to undermine the early modern view of the world: nineteenth-century romanticism, and a few years later, the biology of Charles Darwin, followed then by the philosophy of Friedrich Nietzsche.

Romantic Modernists

The romantics were especially influenced by Hume's and Rousseau's emphasis on feeling and by Kant's emphasis on an active mind that creates its picture of the world. They were also influenced by historical developments such as the emergence of oppressive factory production, miserable workhouses, and big-city slums. As a result of these influences they began a romantic crusade against reason. Specifically, they began insisting that the highest and most needed truths are subjective rather than objective and that these truths can be discovered only through intuition and feeling, not through reason.

Following Rousseau's *Discourse on Inequality* (see *The Social Contract and Discourses*), the romantics argued that the social problems of the nineteenth century stemmed from the influence of a repressive and corrupting civilization that turned human beings away from their natural compassion for others. As Rousseau said, since God is good, He must have created a good human nature, and as long as human beings live in harmony with that nature, their behavior will also be good. The problem is that human beings are now forced to live under the artificial social order which began to develop after the agricultural revolution, a social order based on the notion of private property, and in conforming to this order they begin to ignore their natural goodness. What is needed is to forget books and the "mind-forged manacles" of a rational civilization and to simply "return to nature." Instead of following reason, human beings must get back in touch with their deepest and most private feelings—back to the good, unsocialized part of themselves that exists beneath the surface of civilized reason. If we do this, if we once again let nature be our teacher, a natural benevolence will again rule the human world.

By identifying reason with repression, artificiality, and moral corruption, rather than with freedom, truth, and moral progress, romanticism mounted a loud attack on the modernist faith in reason. But as with Hume, it is easy to overgeneralize the romantic rebellion, for in many ways the romantics continued the modernist project. To begin with, they continued to believe that human beings have a very substantial essential nature—specifically, innate feelings which by themselves could give a moral shape to our lives. The romantics also continued to believe that human beings should strive to discover the truth and that this truth could serve as a foundation for a better world. Truth might now be subjective and felt, rather than objective and reasoned, but it has not lost its modernist importance as the key to salvation. Finally, as is the case with all modernists, language remains in the background of the romantic view of human life. In the foreground there is either a distorted life controlled by civilized reason, or a good life controlled by feelings which arise naturally from the body.

Darwin on the Beauty of Kant's Rose

Publishing just after the middle of the century, Darwin initiated a far more important nineteenth-century attack on the modernist tradition. Perhaps, above all, his *On the Origin of Species* strongly suggests that there is no rational universe to be discovered. In claiming that life has evolved, Darwin emphasizes a blind and pointless struggle. The emergence of a new species of plant or animal has nothing to do with a rational unfolding of a preexisting plan; it is a consequence of nothing more than a series of contingent events, of a history of random mutations or accidents which happened to be selected by changing environmental conditions. And as the variations, or mutations, keep occurring and the environment keeps changing, the new species die out, to be replaced by others—a process that goes on and on, for no apparent reason. Even the beauty of Kant's rose is seen as nothing special; it, too, is just another product of time and chance, of accidental mutations which happened to survive in a pointless, competitive struggle. And the same kind of history explains the emergence of *Homo sapiens,* a species that happened to get an edge over its competitors through its greater cleverness, for no apparent reason.

Whether accurate or not, Darwin's savage picture of nature, backed up by mountains of the kind of evidence that scientists take seriously, made the modernist view of things seem like just another religion, based on faith rather than empirical evidence. In particular, Kant's rational, well-designed universe is nowhere in sight; nor is there any suggestion that a human being is a special, rational kind of animal. Human beings, like all animals, have evolved historically in interaction with their environments, but there is apparently nothing rational about this history. Nor is there any evidence that natural selection favors the emergence of a truth-detecting animal; ants, for example, have been doing quite well for a long time, but it is doubtful that they have developed an objective view of the universe.

In short, after Darwin the whole modernist project of trying to discover the truth about human nature, so that we can live in harmony with it, begins to seem senseless. In taking us back to our natural roots Darwin shows us some apes, power struggles, and nature red in tooth and claw, not Naked Reasoners or Noble Savages. So why should we attempt to be true to our nature? What now seems to count isn't the truth about ourselves, whether derived from reason or feeling, but finding better ways of coping with our surroundings. From a postmodern point of view, this is exactly what we should think about. But Darwin missed something important: that language is the key to human coping.

Nietzsche's Postmodern Stomach

At this point, toward the end of the nineteenth century, Nietzsche enters our story, and he is sometimes seen as the first philosopher to develop a postmodern view of our situation in the world. Like Darwin, Nietzsche pictures human beings as clever animals who are fighting it out in a fierce competitive struggle. But because Nietzsche lacked Darwin's faith in the truth, and also because he began emphasizing the role that language plays in shaping human life, his view of the world is sharply separated from all forms of modernism.

For Nietzsche human beings are neither rational mirrors of nature nor beautiful flower children. Rather, they are wills to power, and, instead of locating truth, what they really want is to increase their control over the world. These creatures reason and try to find knowledge, but only to bend the world to their domineering will to power. Nietzsche tells us that the spirit of these hungry power-seekers can best be compared to a "stomach" (1973, 142)—an organ which is always trying to appropriate and absorb what is different from itself, trying to make the foreign familiar. Rather than taking pleasure in being an accurate, passive mirror of nature, or in just feeling at one with nature, this stomach-spirit finds its greatest pleasure when it is successful in digesting or transforming its surroundings.

For Nietzsche, even the moral thinking of the stomach-spirits is rooted in their will to power. According to one of his most famous examples, powerless Jews and Christians invented a new "slave morality" (1973, 175) in order to overcome their more powerful Roman masters. Specifically, the praise of the weak and the call for pity that we see in the Sermon on the Mount was merely a subtle attempt of the powerless to overcome and control the powerful. In this view, when the failing student asks the teacher to take pity on him, the teacher should interpret this as just another sneaky student power trip. And if the teacher shows pity, it has nothing to do with a categorical imperative or innate feelings of benevolence; rather, one will to power has simply triumphed over another will to power.

It should be noted that Nietzsche's explanation of the origins of Christian morality is not an argument against practicing it, but perhaps the more important postmodern issue is how to interpret Nietzsche's "will to power." Should we think of the desire for power as inevitably tied to interpersonal dominance, as Foucault and Lyotard do, or should we think of it as the desire to create a world, as Rorty does? While there is postmodern disagreement on this particular issue, there is widespread agreement that Nietzsche was right in stressing the connection between power and what passes for "knowledge" in a society.

In describing human beings, Nietzsche argues that it is language, history, and the ability to create new worlds that separate us from other power-seeking animals, not our ability to find truth. With regard to language, Nietzsche is apparently the first Western philosopher to stress that all thought is linguistic, and, furthermore, that language itself imposes a shape on the way human beings think about the world. For example, whereas Kant argued that the concept of a "thing," as opposed to an "event," was produced in consciousness as a result of an innate mental category, Nietzsche argues that it is produced by language. Specifically, when we think about our changing experiences, we do so in sentences which have subjects in addition to predicates, and it this linguistic thinking that leads us to think of the world as divided into things and events. As Nietzsche says, although we only have sensations of a lightning flash—that is, of a single event on the horizon—when we reflect, we "double" (1956, 179) what we were immediately aware of into a thing in addition to the event, thus thinking: "The lightning flashed."

Because we also think about ourselves in language, we similarly double the changing thoughts that we are actually aware of into a self which exists in addition to the changing thoughts—a self which *has* the thoughts. For Nietzsche all things, including atoms as well as selves, are "fictions," and here he is close to Hume. But where Hume argued that the individual imagination creates the fictions, for Nietzsche the "creator" is the public language which has been internalized. This point about the intimate connection between language and organized thought is a major postmodern topic, and it will be more fully developed in the next two sections on Saussure and Wittgenstein and in the following chapter on Rorty.

Like Hegel, Nietzsche regards human beings as historical animals, but whereas Hegel saw history as a rational progression toward truth, Nietzsche did not. He just saw societies as changing their "perspectives" or belief systems over time, but without arriving at more accurate pictures of the world. And as is the case with the postmoderns who follow him, Nietzsche could see nothing special about the linguistic pictures of modern science.

To understand the postmodern Nietzsche it should be noted that Nietzsche began his intellectual life as a philologist. In this role he was typically trying to discover the original text of a Greek play—what Sophocles or Plato had originally said. What he eventually discovered was that he could not get to the original—all he could find were various conflicting copies which had been written down over the centuries. And just as he concluded that a philologist cannot discover Sophocles's original text, so he concluded that the truth-seeker cannot get to the "original text" of nature. The truth-seeker can keep searching, but all he can come up with are various "interpretations," i.e., subjective views of nature rather than an objective copy. Nietzsche even goes so far as to say that the whole idea of pursuing truth is a "mistake," and in his "How the 'Real World' at Last Became a Myth," in *Twilight of the Idols*, he classifies the pursuit of truth as "the history of an error" (1968, 50–51). For Nietzsche "God is dead" means that "truth is dead," and he thinks that we should stop searching for what does not exist.

While a modernist would despair over our inability to locate truth, for Nietzsche it is time to rejoice at getting rid of an artificial "burden." Besides, as Nietzsche says about scholars in *Beyond Good and Evil*, what human being really wants to become an objective "*mirror*" (1973, 115), a bleached-out, passive thing that merely reflects rather than makes the world? Now that truth is dead we are free to drop this flat objective pose and instead direct our energy toward the creation of ourselves and of the world we live in. Although a human being is born into chaos, and although she lacks anything resembling a rational core and is nothing more than a set of competing drives for power, she is still capable of bringing this mess under control and giving "style" to her life. As is revealed by our changing history, a human being is a creature who can overcome her past and give her world an interesting and beautiful order, and for Nietzsche this is what a superwoman should do. In other words, Nietzsche tells us that it is now time to abandon the modernist project, time to forget about original texts and solid foundations. What now counts is not the world we discover but the world we create; as Nietzsche says: "This world can be justified only as an esthetic phenomenon" (1956, 143).

The Fly and the Fly-Bottle: Postmodern Thought about Language from Saussure and Wittgenstein to Barthes and Derrida

As mentioned earlier, to a large extent the modern-postmodern debate is a result of a new way of thinking about language—a way of thinking which first began to appear in the late-nineteenth-century philosophy of Nietzsche and Peirce, but which has especially influenced recent postmodern thought through the twentieth-century linguistic theory of Saussure and the philosophy of Wittgenstein. As we will see in this section, there are two main issues—how we should think about language in general, and how we should think about its relation to human thought. In dealing with these issues, both Saussure and Wittgenstein at first accepted a traditional view that stretches back to Plato and Aristotle, but then rejected it in favor of a postmodern view. At the end of this section, while briefly discussing Barthes and Derrida, we will conclude with some of the radical implications of their later postmodern view.

First, we need to look at the traditional view, which assumes that in learning a language there is a natural order of progression from objects in the world, to thoughts about them, and then to words that express those thoughts: first the objects, then the thoughts, and finally the words, and each is clearly separate from the others. First there was a dog in my yard, then upon noticing it, I had a thought about it, and finally, in order to communicate, I found a word to express the thought.

This traditional way of thinking is common sense for most people, and it has encouraged several conclusions about language. First, it leads to the conclusion that language is essentially a list of names which stand for objects; again, after the objects produce thoughts in us, we find words to stand for them. This traditional view of language is sometimes called "nomenclaturism," and it assumes that the naming relation is the key to language.

Second, each word in a language gets its meaning from standing for an object in the world, or, in a second version, from standing for a mental picture of an object. "Dog" gets its meaning from standing for a particular kind of animal or for a mental picture of this animal. This way of thinking about meaning is sometimes called "the picture theory of meaning," and it encourages a third conclusion about language: that its main function is to describe the objects that we experience. From this it also seems to follow that in an ideal language, the relations of words in a sentence will accurately picture the relations of facts in the world it describes. This is what Wittgenstein argued in his first book on language (see Wittgenstein 1947).

Finally, in the traditional view thought is prior to language. First came the thought about the dog in my yard, and later I found the right word to express my thought. Thinking and speaking are thus seen as two separate activities, the one an activity with ideas, the other an activity with words—and the words do not influence the ideas, according to this traditional view which seems to dominate all modernist thought. To use a more important example, my thoughts about light and dark skin precede and are not influenced by how the people around me describe light and dark skin.

Although this traditional view also dominated the early thought of Saussure and Wittgenstein, they later replaced it with a postmodern view. To begin with, instead of thinking of language as a list of names which stand for objects, both writers began thinking of language as a "game" (Wittgenstein 1958, 5) that human beings play, a self-contained game with rules which allow some moves but not others, like chess. Thus Wittgenstein says that "the question 'What is a word really?' is analogous to 'What is a piece in chess'" (Kenney 1994, 281), and he also says that saying "I can use the word 'yellow'" is like "I know how to move the king in chess" (Wittgenstein 1974, 49). In taking this game approach, Wittgenstein de-emphasized the naming relation in language, and he pointed out that many words do not bring pictures to mind—e.g., "is," "ought," "no"—and yet they obviously have meaning for us.

Furthermore, both Wittgenstein and Saussure eventually argued that words get their meaning not from their relation to objects in the world, but from the other words in the language game that they are a part of; it is the total linguistic system that determines the meaning of its individual parts, not their relation to something outside the system. For example, the word "yellow" does not get its meaning from standing for a color that exists independently in the world, for the color spectrum is a continuum rather than a series of independent colors. Rather, "yellow" gets its meaning from the linguistic system that is imposed on the spectrum and that arbitrarily divides it into various colors. In other words, it gets its meaning from a system of "differences" that separates yellow from not-yellow, e.g., from "red" and "green," and not from its relation to an independent object in the world. As Wittgenstein said, "The sign (the sentence) gets its significance from the system of signs, from the language to which it belongs" (1969, 5), or as he later put it, the meaning of a word is determined by its "use" (1974, 60).

The later Wittgenstein also began emphasizing something which should have been obvious but which philosophers had ignored: that we use words for several different purposes—to make promises, to convey emotion, to improve moral behavior—and not just to describe or picture the world. He didn't deny that we sometimes use words to describe the world, but he did deny that this is the only or the primary function of language. Thus he tells us to drop the idea that language is a set of pictures, and instead to think of it as a "box of tools" that we use to accomplish a variety of objectives.

In taking this approach to language, the later Wittgenstein moved away from the philosopher's concern with the picturing or referential function of language, but he went even further and began arguing that it doesn't make sense to think that any language or description gives us an accurate picture of the world, no matter how logically precise or scientific. As he says, "A *picture* held us captive. And we could not get outside it, for it lay in our language and language seemed to repeat it to us inexorably" (1958, 48). His point here is not that *some* languages give us a false picture of the world, but that there is no reason to think that *any* language gives us an accurate one. Why should we think that a human-made language is a picture of nature? This issue of whether we ever arrive at accurate pictures of the world runs throughout postmodern thought, and we will discuss it more fully in the next chapter on Richard Rorty.

But first it should be noted that both Saussure and Wittgenstein also reversed traditional ideas about the priority of thought to language. In their later view, we don't have thoughts about objects prior to the internalization of language. Prior to language—a system which organizes and describes and judges the world—there is a world of changing sensation, but not an organized system of concepts. The latter, the world of conceptual thought, develops under the guidance of a language which causes us to separate out objects and events from the flow of experience. Thus in a famous passage Wittgenstein says:

> When I think in language there aren't meanings going through my mind in addition to the verbal expressions; the language itself is the vehicle of thought. (1974, 161)

In other words, it doesn't make sense to talk about a deep, independent layer of thought which underlies language; thought and language are interdependent. Of course, there is a brain which exists independent of language, but it is not a brain with concepts. As Saussure says:

> Just as it is impossible to take a pair of scissors and cut one side of a paper without at the same time cutting the other, so it is impossible in a language to separate sound from thought, or thought from sound. (1974, 157)

This view of the interdependence of language and thought has several implications that are at the center of postmodernism. First, without language there is no organized conceptual thought. On the possibility of prelinguistic thought, Saussure says:

> Psychologically, setting aside its expression in words, our thought is simply a vague shapeless mass. No ideas are established in advance, and nothing is distinct, before the introduction of linguistic structure. (1983, 155)

Wittgenstein doesn't seem to go quite this far, and he suggests that perhaps a dog does have the thought that his master is at the door, but then he quickly asks: "Can the dog also have the thought that his master will return the day after tomorrow?" (1958, 174). And he further suggests that the dog could not hope for his master's future arrival: "Only those who have mastered the use of language" can hope (1958, 174). It is also difficult to believe that a dog could have many thoughts about the door itself—e.g., that it is five years old; that it was made for a particular purpose; that because of certain causal relations, it will one day no longer exist; that it is composed of tiny particles called atoms; that it is a well-made door; that it belongs in a different part of the room; that it is a beautiful door. Thus, while the dog becomes aware of various sensations from the door, these sensations are followed by few, if any, rudimentary thoughts about it.

For postmoderns the same would be true of a human being who had not internalized language. In *Seeing Voices*, this claim is strongly supported by neurologist Oliver Sacks. Sacks specifically describes the mental life of older deaf children who had never had the opportunity to learn a language (including sign language), and what he emphasizes is that they live in a mental world of particulars and concrete images, rather than in a language-user's generalized world of abstract concepts.

This postmodern point that thought is essentially linguistic has other implications that undermine a modernist view of the world. For one thing, it suggests that it no longer makes sense to talk about Descartes's isolated, self-sufficient thinker—about an isolated "I" that thinks. Since all organized thought is in language, and since language is a public creation, it follows that an individual's thought is essentially public and social. Of course, we can't see into one another's heads, but since the vehicle of thought is a public language, thinking is basically a public rather than a private activity. In this view an individual's thoughts no longer originate in the individual; the center is now located in the collective language game that has taken over the individual's head. And if this is the case, it is even possible to drop the modernist idea that an individual speaks a language and to instead accept Heidegger's claim that "language speaks" man.

In other words, if we accept the idea that language is prior to thought, we will also reject the modernist idea that the self is "expressed" by language. Instead we will see the self as "created" by language. Specifically, we will assume that the beliefs and desires that mark off an individual human being enter her head under the guidance of a collective language—that it is language rather than nature that puts her self together. Since it gives the human being her beliefs, desires, and emotions (which will be discussed in Chapter 5), Heidegger can say that it "speaks" her. Notice that this view of the self doesn't deny that human beings are also influenced by their bodies and private life histories, but it emphasizes that these nonlinguistic factors are inevitably mediated by the organizing collective weight of a community language. Here it should also be noted that the need for successful collective action will cause all communities to place great limits on rule-breaking uses of language. As in chess, if the pieces in the language game are moved in defiance of the traditional rules, if kids are allowed to use words every which way, the game breaks down, and so does the community life based on it. We will discuss linguistic deviance and metaphor in the next chapter; here the main point is that if thought is linguistic, we should drop the modernist notion of a private, independent, and encapsulated self.

Postmodern writers such as Barthes and Derrida were among the first to draw out some of these radical implications of a Saussurean-Wittgensteinian view of language and thought. In his famous essay "The Death of the Author," Barthes tells teachers and literary critics that it is time to drop the idea that an author gives a literary work its meaning. Echoing Heidegger, Barthes says "it is language which speaks, not the author" (1992, 115), and thus he also tells us that we should drop the project of trying to explain a text by referring to the author who wrote it—specifically, to an author's original intentions, passions, tastes, life, or anything else that exists outside of language. Instead of thinking of Shakespeare as an author who "expressed" his "self" in *Hamlet*, Barthes tells us to think of Shakespeare as a "scriptor" who expressed:

> a ready-formed dictionary, its words explainable through other words, and so on indefinitely. . . . Succeeding the Author, the scriptor no longer bears within him passions, humors, feelings, impressions, but rather this immense dictionary from which he draws a writing that can know no halt: life never does more than imitate the book [language], and the book itself is only a tissue of signs, an imitation that is lost, infinitely deferred. (1992, 117)

Barthes concludes by saying that the death of the author is a liberating event because without an author, there is no secret and ultimate meaning to get hung up on, no final message which the critic has discovered and the individual reader must accept. For if the author doesn't exist independently of language, the individual reader becomes the source of whatever meaning the text has, and she is now left free to make her own interpretation. In *Writing and Difference*, Derrida develops a similar view of a text's meaning, and he, too, tells us to rejoice in the absence of a discoverable once-and-for-all meaning, for without it, each individual is left free to "play" with a text, free to make it mean whatever serves today's needs and interests. As Derrida says, with the "absent origin" (1989, 164), it becomes possible to embrace

> . . . the Nietzschean *affirmation,* that is, the joyous affirmation of the play of the world and of the innocence of becoming, the affirmation of a world of signs without fault, without truth, and without origin which is offered an active interpretation. (164)

For Derrida as for Barthes, readers can now forget about the old burden of trying to capture what an author was "really trying to say" and instead focus joyfully on the meaning they create in interpreting a text. In other words, the insubstantial pageant is all there is, and what counts now is the play in which language is spun into a beautiful shape.

Here it should be noted that this postmodern view of interpretation is supported by Wittgenstein's later claim that language is the inevitable vehicle of thought—that there is no way to break outside of language while continuing to think about the world in an organized way. As Wittgenstein put it, the thinking human being is a "fly [trapped inside the] fly-bottle," always buzzing around within the limits of a human-made language. But the fly's situation leads not only to doubts about the project of locating an author's "true meaning"; it also leads to doubts about the entire project of discovering justified true beliefs about the world. As Wittgenstein argued in *On Certainty,* we can never fully justify our beliefs, and "at the foundation of well-founded belief lies belief that is not founded" (Kenney 1994, 257). In other words, it is time to follow Nietzsche's advice and bury Descartes's search for a solid foundation and eternal truth.

At least that's what the later Wittgenstein concluded, and as a result he changed his approach to philosophy. As a young man he followed modernist Bertrand Russell and adopted a scientific and logical approach, closely analyzing language in order to get at the truth about the world. But after reaching his later postmodern conclusions, he gave up on the attempt to solve philosophical problems and find truth. In his later philosophy he continued to analyze language, but his new goal became therapeutic, and he simply wanted to dissolve problems (1958, 47). In this later view philosophy becomes "a battle against the bewitchment of our intelligence by means of language" (47).

To see the significance of Wittgenstein's later "therapy," it is convenient to put philosophy aside and to think about social or personal problems. To begin with, if we have such problems—say, in getting along with other racial or ethnic groups—the immediate cause of the problem is not something objective that lies outside of the language we think in. Since we're all flies trapped inside a fly-bottle, our problems stem from the nature of our fly-bottles, i.e., from the descriptions of the world that we think in and live under. And if this is the case, what we need to worry about isn't whether the descriptions are true—which, since we can never break out of the fly-bottle, we can never know anyway—but rather what the descriptions are like, how they influence our thought and behavior, and how they should be changed to solve our problems. At this point we can begin to see the pragmatic as well as the creative side of postmodernism, and in the next chapter we will turn to the American postmodern pragmatist Richard Rorty.

2 Richard Rorty's Postmodern Synthesis

There are a number of major postmodern writers—Heidegger, Gadamer, Derrida, Lyotard, Foucault, Jameson, and Baudrillard are among the most important—but in our opinion, philosopher Richard Rorty provides the most important postmodern view of our situation in the world. Rorty's major works include *Philosophy and the Mirror of Nature* (1980); *Consequences of Pragmatism* (1982); *Contingency, Irony, and Solidarity* (1989); *Objectivity, Relativism, and Truth* (1991a); and *Essays on Heidegger and Others* (1991b). He writes in a clear, democratic style which is open to the nonspecialist. In *Philosophy and the Mirror of Nature*, Rorty argues that philosophers should above all attempt to carry on a "conversation with mankind" (1980, 389), and in all of his books and articles he seems to be carrying on a conversation with just about everybody, inside and outside of philosophy, who has an idea on a postmodern theme. A reader new to postmodern thought will quickly learn the various positions of other postmoderns, and Rorty's constant dialogue with other major writers is one of the more appealing aspects of his style. But most important, Rorty establishes a connection between postmodernism and American pragmatism, and it is this connection which makes his postmodern philosophy especially valuable.

The Ubiquity of Language

In analyzing the situation of human beings in the world, Rorty follows the later Saussure and Wittgenstein in emphasizing that language provides the starting point for all organized conceptual thought about the world. As he says in *Consequences of Pragmatism:*

> . . . attempts to get back behind language to something that "grounds" it, or that it "expresses," or to which it might hope to be "adequate," have not worked. The ubiquity of language is a matter of language moving into the vacancies left by the failure of all the various candidates for the position of "natural starting points" of thought, starting points that are prior to and independent of the way some culture speaks or spoke. (Candidates for such starting points include clear and distinct ideas, sense data, categories of the

> pure understanding, structures of prelinguistic consciousness, and the like.) (1982, *xx*)

Here it should be stressed that in denying all starting points of thought other than "the way some cultures speak or spoke," Rorty is not denying that babies first have private, prelinguistic sensations. What he is denying is that such sensations or "raw feels" provide the basis for an older child's conceptual thought and knowledge-claims about the world. Specifically, Rorty is not denying that babies first experience a changing swirl of color, but only that this private swirl provides the basis for later distinctions, as when the child starts saying "that's red, not orange." Thus, while not ignoring sensations prior to language, Rorty posits a sharp break in a child's mental life—a break that takes place with the internalization of a community language at about the age of three or four. Only after this event takes place is the child capable of the organized conceptual thought that enables him to make knowledge claims such as "that's red, not orange" or "that's a dog, not a cat."

In emphasizing the "ubiquity of language" Rorty is also claiming that a human being cannot later set aside her internalized language while continuing to think conceptually about the world. As Rorty says, "I cannot think of thinking as something different from using language" (Saatkamp 1995, 123), or more succinctly, "language goes all the way down" (1982, *x–xx*). In other words, Wittgenstein was right in claiming that human thinkers remain forever trapped within their linguistic fly-bottles.

Mind as a "Mirror of Nature"?

But human beings tend to ignore this and act as though they could see outside the fly-bottle, and if they go to a modern school they will be encouraged to think of knowledge as an accurate representation of what is outside—an accurate representation of nature ("modern school" = a school under the influence of Descartes and the modern epistemologically centered philosophy discussed in the previous chapter). In such a school the student will be told that human beings should strive to acquire more accurate pictures of nature, and she will also be told that philosophy teachers are experts at finding out which pictures are accurate and which are not. In other words, the student will be told that philosophy teachers can know what is outside the fly-bottle.

Like the later Wittgenstein, Rorty cannot make sense of this modern way of thinking, and thus he wants us to abandon the search for increasingly accurate pictures of nature. In his first book, *Philosophy and the Mirror of Nature,* he claims that what gave sense to the search in the past was a metaphor which was popular throughout the modern era—the metaphor of the mind as "a mirror of nature." As Rorty says in introducing the history of modern philosophy:

> It is pictures rather than propositions, metaphors rather than statements, which determine most of our philosophical convictions. The picture which holds traditional philosophy captive is that of the mind as a great mirror, containing various representations—some accurate, some not—and capable of being studied by pure, nonempirical methods. Without the notion of the mind as mirror, the notion of knowledge as accuracy of representation would not have suggested itself. Without this latter notion, the strategy common to Descartes and Kant—getting more accurate representations by inspecting, repairing, and polishing the mirror, so to speak—would not have made sense. Without this strategy in mind, recent claims that philosophy could consist of "conceptual analysis," of "phenomenological analysis," or "explication of meanings," or the examination of "the logic of our language" or "the structure of the constituting activity of consciousness" would not have made sense. It was such claims as these which Wittgenstein mocked in the *Philosophical Investigations.* . . .
> (1980, 12)

In *Measure for Measure,* Shakespeare called this "great mirror" of nature our "glassy essence" (2.2.117–23), and throughout the modern era, it was assumed that our ability to mirror nature was what set us apart from the other animals. And if Rorty is right in his analysis of the history of philosophy, the same mirror imagery is what inspired the modern project of representing nature accurately—the project of studying the mirror closely with the mind's eye in order to find nature's true reflections in it. In tracing the history of this philosophy, which confused knowledge with visual perception, Rorty concludes with a discussion of the twentieth-century shift from thinking of the mirror's mental reflections (ideas or images) to thinking of its linguistic reflections (sentences). But while he is sympathetic to this "linguistic turn," he also argues that it cannot save the project of modern philosophy, for there is no reason to believe that human beings have anything resembling mirrors of nature in their heads. We do have brains, apparently shaped by the process of natural selection, but a human brain doesn't seem to be like a "glassy essence" which can be studied by a mind's eye. And as Rorty says, if we are "no longer held captive" by such mirror imagery, we will no longer be tempted to think that human beings can arrive at accurate representations of nature.

If teachers followed Rorty's postmodern discussion of representation, we would no longer encourage our students to think of "knowledge" as a belief which is acquired through a direct confrontation between what is in the mind and what is in nature. Rather, we would say that what we call knowledge is determined by "conversation." Specifically, we would think of knowledge as an assertion which no one around us wants to question. When we say, "grass is green" or "force equals mass times acceleration," and everybody around says, "no doubt about it," we think we have arrived at knowledge, but our certainty in such matters is not a result of a confrontation between what is in the "great mirror" and what is in nature. As Rorty puts it in a more recent essay, "our sense of . . . objectivity is not a matter of corresponding to objects, but of getting together with other subjects— . . . there is nothing to objectivity except intersubjectivity" (1994, 56).

Truth?

In a world without mental mirrors, what should teachers tell their students about "truth"? Rorty's answer is the same in all of his later writings: tell them that "we should drop the topic" (e.g., 1982, *xiii–xiv*). To see why, we need to be more specific. To begin with, in making this comment Rorty is thinking of truth as it is normally defined, by common sense as well as by Plato—truth as a belief or description of the world that corresponds to the way the world actually is. Technically, this is called the "correspondence theory of truth"—where "correspondence" is synonymous with "represents or pictures the world accurately." Thus the description "the sky is blue" is true if the sky is, in fact, blue, false if it is not, just as the belief or description "I have an innate feeling of benevolence for all human beings" is true if I do, false if I don't.

In his discussion of correspondence theory, Rorty points to the same basic problem that Wittgenstein, Nietzsche, Hume, and Berkeley saw, but his analysis is much more sharply focused; and since this issue goes to the heart of postmodernism, we need to look at it closely. The problem is that it is impossible to determine if a belief or description accurately represents the world as it exists independent of thought. To see why this is a problem, we need to remember that "the sky is blue" is a description that exists in my head when I think about the sky, whereas the actual sky is something that exists in the outside world. In trying to discover truth there are thus two factors involved: the linguistic description that I think in, and the world outside. There is no doubt about what the description says, but to determine its truth I would have to compare what it says with the objective sky to see if they match. The problem is that in order to make such a comparison, I would have to slip outside my mind and language and confront the objective sky directly, and since there is no way to do this, I have no way of finding out whether the description is true. I can compare the present description with other descriptions, as when I remember what the sky looked like last night or through my sunglasses, but as a fly in the fly-bottle I cannot set aside all descriptions and directly encounter an objective, undescribed sky. Nor can I detect the correspondence between "force equals mass times acceleration" and whatever else exists in the world.

Here it should be emphasized that this argument is not denying that *something* exists in the world outside of the descriptions we think in. It is not denying that there is an objective universe which is as it is regardless of how we describe it. What is being denied is that it makes sense to talk about *something else* which is also objective and called "truth."

In taking this position on truth, Rorty repeatedly emphasizes that we have no reason to think that the language of modern science is somehow unique when it comes to corresponding to the world. This position sharply separates Rorty from Galileo, who at the beginning of the modern era argued that the new mathematical language of science was special because "the book of nature is written in the language of mathematics." But as Rorty says, there is no reason to think that nature is written in mathematics or in any other language (e.g., 1982, 191–95). This isn't to deny that scientific descriptions do enable us to make more accurate predictions and also to gain greater control over nature, but predictability and control differ from an accurate picture of nature. Why should we ever infer that a language we made can accurately describe a nature that we didn't make? Indeed, it is quite possible that prediction and control are made possible only by a language which misrepresents what actually exists in nature.

If you disagree with this position on science, if you think that the mathematical language of modern physics does correspond, are you assuming that our human-made equations are somehow "in" the external world? Perhaps they are, and perhaps there are atoms out there, and perhaps Zeus is out there—but we have no way of climbing outside of our linguistic minds to find out. Nor is there any way of finding out the truth about why the teacher murdered the students who slept in class, whether it was "because of killer genes" or "because of an unresolved Oedipus complex" or "because the Devil made him do it" or whether it was "out of his own free will." As Hume showed, we cannot discover truth about any causal relations. Since Hume's day, philosophers and scientists have been struggling to disprove him, but they haven't even been able to establish whether all causes are material, or mental, or whether there are perhaps two kinds of causes which explain what happens in the universe.

Here we might ask ourselves whether English teachers should give up on the intent to discover the true meaning of a literary work. Is there any reason to believe that through literary scholarship and historical knowledge we can arrive at what an author was really trying to say—his "original intention"? For Rorty, as for Barthes and Derrida, the answer is no, and thus he, too, tells us to "forget the question of whether one has got its [the text's] 'meaning' or 'the author's intention'" (Mitchell 1985, 134). Rorty emphasizes that as our fly-bottles change over time, so do our interpretations of a text's meaning—as is classically illustrated in the various interpretations of *Hamlet*. But he also emphasizes that there is no reason to believe that the later interpretations are more "accurate" than the earlier ones.

To conclude this attack on truth, we should not think that there is something special about the discovery of one's "true self." For Rorty, there is no reason to suppose that an introspecting human being has a direct view into her self (or mind), for here, too, "language goes all the way down." In other words, the same problem arises, and whenever I introspect and think about what I "really am," I directly encounter nothing but various descriptions of what I am—e.g., "an animal with free will," "a rational essence," "a lump of atoms," "a creature who has a natural compassion for all human beings," etc. And since I am never directly aware of an undescribed reality which exists beneath these descriptions, I can never know the truth about "the real me." In this view people who tell us that they have "found themselves" have found nothing more than a particular description in their heads which they have faith in. But as between language and the external world, the gap between language and the inner world cannot be crossed, which is why it is pointless to talk about whether one has been true to herself.

On first reading this analysis of truth, it might be easy to conclude that Rorty's postmodern philosophy is just another example of intellectual nihilism. But this isn't the case, and to see why we need to look at some of the conclusions which Rorty draws from his negative discussion of truth. We have already mentioned that he wants us to drop the topic, but he doesn't stop there, and his main concern is to shift our intellectual focus from worrying about what is true to worrying about what works in getting us what we want. If we were to make this shift, we would stop worrying about whether literature, philosophy, and science are giving us accurate pictures of the world, and instead focus on what they help us accomplish, just as we do with our other tools. All language, in this Wittgensteinian view, should be seen as a tool that we use to solve problems rather than as an accurate picture of the world,

and in this respect the language of philosophy is no different from the
language of literature.

Rorty's Postmodern Utopia

In *Contingency, Irony, and Solidarity,* Rorty presents his ideas about utopia, and while looking at the positive side of his thought, we can contrast these ideas to Plato's ideas about utopia in *The Republic.* To begin
with, Plato's utopia—we could call it the first modern utopia—is devoted to truth. It is a society in which people are encouraged to seek out
eternal essences and moral truths and to then base their lives on them. It
is also a society in which individuals are tightly controlled and in which
there is little room for diversity. Universal Man is welcome, but not the
Other; and individual lives are to be governed by reason and the general rules that all rational animals should follow, rather than by private
desires and the individual imagination. Near the end of *The Republic*
Plato even tells us that the artist would be banished from utopia because his imaginative descriptions stimulate emotion and prevent reason from discovering truth. At the top of the power hierarchy is the philosopher-king, and he dictates because he is the most rational truth-finder,
and therefore knows what's best for everybody. Despite his rational approach to life, Plato's philosopher-king does not see our relation to the
Other as a special moral problem.

The contrast: Rorty's postmodern utopia in *Contingency* is a democratic society devoted to freedom, creativity, and the reduction of cruelty. "Freedom" here means the freedom to create and live in terms of
one's idiosyncratic fantasies without obsessing on truth and the universal rules that all rational beings should follow. Rorty's utopia is thus a
society which is open to change and diversity, a society in which citi-
zens are encouraged to follow their personal desires and fantasies while
creating themselves in new and interesting ways. Individual freedom
rather than the reign of universal truth would be the major political preoccupation in this postmodern utopia, and the Other would be welcome.
As Rorty says, "If we take care of political freedom, truth and goodness
will take care of themselves" (1989, 84). In such a society, what people
come to believe would be determined by a free exchange of ideas, by
persuasion in an open democracy, rather than by force.

Rorty's postmodern utopia would thus be a "poeticized" rather than
a "rationalized" or "scientized" utopia (1989, 53), and the poet and the
creator would be the major cultural heroes, rather than the philosopher,

scientist, or any other pretentious truth-finder. Science would still be around, for we would still need to solve the problems of food production and tooth decay, but science would not be seen as the most important human activity. Nor would it be seen as giving us a language which describes the world accurately—a language which everybody should strive to copy because it gives us truth. In other words, "physics-envy will become less prevalent, and . . . distinctions between disciplines will no longer be drawn in phallogocentric terms, such as hard and soft" (1994, 55).

Finally, the ideal citizen in Rorty's utopia would be preoccupied with self-creation rather than with self-discovery, but this private concern for creating and perfecting one's self would be balanced by a public concern for human solidarity and moral improvement. This ideal citizen would be what Rorty calls a "liberal ironist" (1989, *xv*)—where "ironist" means someone who lives with the thought that no beliefs can be rationally justified, someone who realizes that neither she nor anyone else will ever know the truth about the world. By "liberal" Rorty means someone who believes that "cruelty is the worst thing we do" (*xv*) and whose moral and political behavior is motivated by a strong desire to reduce his own and his society's cruelties.

True Sentences versus a Good Vocabulary

In thinking about Rorty's postmodern utopia, it should first be obvious that the imaginative poet and the creator are the stars, while the rational philosopher and the scientist—the modern stars—get only minor roles. In justifying this reversal Rorty makes a "distinction between finding out whether a proposition is true and finding out whether a vocabulary is good" (1982, 142)—where a "good" vocabulary is defined as one which "will get us what we want" (150).

It is clear that for modernists what counts is true sentences, but Rorty sides with the pragmatists' view that what counts is good vocabulary, "new ways of speaking" that will "help get us what we want" (1982, 150). This position makes sense not only because we can never know whether our sentences are true, but also because language "goes all the way down." In other words, since all thought is linguistic, the vocabulary used to describe an object controls how we think about it—about, say, women, dark skin, homosexuality, or nature in general. From this it follows that if we improve our ways of describing these objects, we will improve how we think about them. A good vocabulary thus becomes all-important in human life, especially if Rorty is right when he claims that "anything could be made to look good or bad, important or unimportant, useful or useless, by being redescribed" (1989, 7).

Poets and Creative Redescribers

With this claim in mind, we should look at Rorty's ideas about the vocabulary of the poet and of the creative writer. Why should their descriptions of the world be ranked above those of the philosopher in a postmodern utopia? Here Rorty emphasizes two points: first, in describing the world, the poet and creative writer rely on concrete images and specific details, and thus they center our attention on particular situations in the world rather than on what is supposedly universal. Second, they take pride in coming up with original descriptions of the world (1991b, 66–82; 1982, 139–43).

Rorty develops this point by contrasting the language of literature with that of normal science. The normal scientist (as against the few geniuses such as Darwin and Newton) uses words in a strict and denotative way, which is essential for scientific precision and for reaching agreement with other scientists. Since metaphor, irony, and, in general, old words used in new ways prevent precision and agreement, there is no room for them in normal science. For example, if in writing up a lab report a student were to say that "the gas rose like Jesus rose from the dead," his science teacher would not classify him as a great scientist. But if he wrote the same thing in a story about a student who couldn't pass science, he might be praised in his English class. The difference is that the English teacher wants to encourage good creative writing, and she knows that it is precisely such unique descriptions that make one a successful creative writer. If Salinger, for example, hadn't described growing up and adolescence in a new way, we wouldn't praise *The Catcher in the Rye*. And if Beckett hadn't come up with the original image of two babbling tramps waiting for Salvation on a road to nowhere, we wouldn't praise his existential description of modern humanity's relation to the world in *Waiting for Godot*. These literary descriptions of the world lack the precision necessary for scientific agreement, but their originality enables human beings to see the world in a new and sometimes better way.

In his essay "Heidegger, Kundera, and Dickens" (1991b, 65–82) and throughout *Contingency, Irony, and Solidarity*, Rorty stresses that the creative writer's novel and concrete way of using language is needed in utopia for several reasons. First, its novelty plays a major role in freeing us from our pasts, from social and personal childhoods which have created problems, cruelty, and suffering. Here it should again be noted that since thought is controlled by language, human problems are inevitably rooted in that language, often in traditional tribal descriptions of the world. We need the poets and creative redescribers because, by reminding us that there are many different ways of describing the world, their novel descriptions free us from the normal tendency to think that there is only One Natural or Right Description. We also need them because some of their novel descriptions—e.g., "Black is beautiful"—replace the old descriptions, and in doing so they foster new ways of thinking which can solve the problems created by the old descriptions. Of course, philosophers have also reminded us of the arbitrary nature of symbolic descriptions, but because of their emphasis on reason and finding the One Right Description, they play down the importance of finding alternative, imaginative ways of describing the world.

Poets and creative redescribers are also important because they serve as inspiration for our private projects of self-perfection. Here we need to remember that for Rorty self-perfection does not come through self-discovery. Rather, self-perfection means self-creation—and since the self is an "incarnated vocabulary," self-perfection means self-redescription. It means finding new and interesting ways to describe oneself and one's situation in the world. In *Contingency*, Rorty singles out Nietzsche, Yeats, Proust, and Derrida as writers who managed to make themselves into something new and interesting through self-redescription, and he thinks the rest of us should do the same. The poet can serve as our inspiration because her novel metaphors and idiosyncratic language remind us that we don't have to remain a copy or clone trapped inside a self-description imposed by a tribe, parent, peer group, or media talk show. She is important because she reminds us that it is possible to escape from our pasts, specifically, from a "self" we never made—possible to give ourselves a more fulfilling and aesthetically interesting shape by coming up with our own self-redescription and then living by it. In a world without truth, a world in which people would face up to the impossibility of ever "finding themselves," the poet and creative redescriber remind us that Nietzsche was right when he said that "this world can be justified only as an esthetic phenomenon" (1956, 143).

Moral Progress and the Reduction of Cruelty

But for Rorty, a private aesthetics isn't the whole story, and thus there is another reason for his desire to make the poet and the creative redescriber our major cultural heroes: their language is essential for increasing human solidarity and reducing cruelty. While Plato and the moderns who followed him tended to think that such moral progress is possible only through reasoning and the discovery of moral truths, Rorty argues that when human beings come together, it is because of an imaginative description of Us and the Other (1989, *xvi*).

With regard to the reduction of human cruelty, Rorty argues that there is a major problem with philosophers' abstract moral theories because they typically fail to direct our attention to the situations where we are actually cruel in everyday life. For example, while searching for Kant's eternal moral truths in his *Fundamental Principles of the Metaphysic of Morals,* while reasoning our way through his "fundamental principles of morality," we are not focusing on the daily situations in which our behavior is cruel—such as when we ignore our relations with our mates or our obligations to America's hopeless ghettos.

As Rorty says, we will reduce our cruelty only if we face it, and here we can see the problem with Kant's abstract and rational approach to moral improvement. For Kant emphasizes that moral thought is essentially a matter of deducing how we ought to act from universal principles; it is simply a matter of reasoning out what our general moral obligations are to other rational beings in all situations. The problem with Kant's approach is that it separates morality from the ability to notice and identify with the humiliation and suffering of the people around us. As noted in the previous chapter, a follower of Kant focuses his attention on whether the categorical imperative would permit him to tell a lie in *any* situation, and thus he can ignore the painful consequences of telling the truth in *this* situation.

For Rorty, the poet, the novelist, and the journalist are more likely to point us in the right direction. Lacking the philosopher's interest in a universal and eternal moral theory, these creative writers focus our attention on specific, everyday cases of cruelty, and thus they are more likely to make us see and feel the humiliation and suffering that we inflict on others.

In addition to making us look in the right direction, creative describers provide the most persuasive redescriptions of cruel situations. These redescriptions are essential to moral progress because our cruelty is the result of our traditional ways of describing ourselves and others. Above all, we typically describe the "others" as different from "us": "Yes, there is a problem in hopeless, violent, and doped-up housing projects, but that's because the blacks are not like us; they are just born with a welfare mentality." Given this description of the situation, few of "us" want to do much to change things. And at this point we can see the importance of the creative writer's redescriptions, for they are essential to changing our thinking about an ugly and cruel situation. Specifically, if a redescription causes us to think that a person who is suffering is "one of us"—e.g., "another mother who wants the best for her child"—we will want to eliminate her pain and hopeless condition.

In putting down Kant's rational approach to moral life, Rorty's main point is that the logical space from which our moral reasoning begins is created by our traditional descriptions of the world, and as he says in "Feminism and Pragmatism," it is these descriptions that typically block moral progress. For example, if "sodomy" is described as a "bestial act," we of course will reason that we should prosecute human beings who practice it. If, on the other hand, we define it as "another act of love that some human beings go in for," then we will start thinking that sodomy laws violate the right to private sexual freedom. This idea that moral reasoning never occurs in a vacuum, that it is always based on a particular description of reality which shapes its conclusions, is one of Rorty's strongest arguments, and it helps to explain why the imaginative redescriber is essential for moral progress.

Rorty especially singles out novelists for making moral progress possible. In *Contingency*, he praises Orwell for his redescription of communism as cruelty and Nabokov for showing us that it is our lack of curiosity about others that helps to explain why it is easy for us to humiliate them. In *Essays on Heidegger and Others*, Rorty especially discusses the nineteenth-century novels of Charles Dickens, and he asks us to think of "the novel, and particularly the novel of moral protest, rather than the philosophical treatise, as the genre in which the West excelled" (1991b, 68). In developing this point Rorty contrasts Dickens with Heidegger, and he argues that a democratic utopia needs Dickens more than it needs philosophers.

Specifically, Rorty argues that a Dickens novel helps to create a democratic society in which there is freedom, equality, and tolerance—a society in which diverse human beings are comfortable with each other. For unlike the typical philosophical treatise, which tries to penetrate beneath particular appearance to universal truth and therefore encourages us to think that there is only One Right Description of the world, the work of Dickens and other novelists focuses our attention on a diversity of viewpoints—without insisting that there is only one privileged, "true" viewpoint. Novelists typically mock the upholder of the single, true viewpoint, as Voltaire mocked Leibniz in *Candide*. In other words, novelists tell us to drop the thought that there is only One Truth (which, of course, is always on "our side"), and they also tell us to take pride in our ability to shift back and forth between different viewpoints. Thus the novel encourages us to be tolerant and open and to find comfort with any old freak, like the freaks in Dickens's novels.

Finally, instead of giving us a grand theory of moral truth, novelists give us a great deal of concrete detail about just who is suffering and where and why. As Rorty concludes: "When you weigh the good and the bad the social novelists have done, against the good and the bad the social theorists have done, you find yourself wishing that there had been more novels and fewer theories" (1991b, 80). Obviously, there have been tolerant philosophers and intolerant novelists, but perhaps, in general, Rorty is right in insisting that the novel has done more for democratic pluralism than philosophy.

Perhaps he is also right when he says about Bosnia that "the emergence of human rights culture seems to owe nothing to increased moral knowledge and everything to hearing sad and sentimental stories" (1993a, 7) like *Uncle Tom's Cabin*. In this same essay, "Human Rights, Rationality, and Sentimentality," Rorty also emphasizes that despite the role of such stories in manipulating moral feelings of sympathy, there are other forces which help to explain a society's moral behavior. In particular, when poverty and insecurity support a traditional description of our enemy, we are not likely to be receptive to a new sad and sentimental story about him. In other words, although the way we think about each other is under the immediate control of how we describe each other, this doesn't mean that we should ignore nonlinguistic factors in trying to explain and change these descriptions. Rorty is not a linguistic idealist.

A Pragmatist's Brand of Postmodernism

In concluding this discussion of Rorty's postmodern utopia and ideas about moral progress, a few other points should be touched upon. First, Rorty's utopia is not a socialist utopia, and it rests on market-based production. Here Rorty is not advocating total laissez-faire, but he thinks we need to face the fact that twentieth-century socialism has been a terrible failure and that we now have no workable alternative to a system which generates an "ethic of greed" (1992). As he says in "The Intellectuals at the End of Socialism," we are stuck with a capitalist society in which "public virtue . . . is going to be parasitic on private vices" (1992).

Although few, if any, postmoderns will defend twentieth-century communism, not all agree with Rorty's willingness to defend Western liberal democracies. Rorty specifically claims that during the past 300 years, liberal democracies—with institutions such as free elections, a free press, an independent judiciary, and public education—have reduced cruelty in the world, and he also claims that these democracies continue to be the best vehicle for moral progress. In taking this position, Rorty disagrees sharply with postmoderns such as Foucault and Lyotard, who would never follow him in referring to themselves as "postmodern bourgeois liberals" (1991b, 199). As we will see in later chapters, Foucault and Lyotard picture democratic societies as little more than restrictive "disciplinary societies" which are "terror" for the Other, and thus they refuse to defend them.

In dealing with the politics of Lyotard and Foucault, Rorty doesn't deny that democratic societies are filled with injustice and inequality, and he doesn't deny that there is a continuing problem with the Other, or that Foucault is right in claiming that in the modern era there has been an increase in "normalizing" restrictions on individual behavior. But he also points out that "you would never guess, from Foucault's account of the changes in European institutions during the last 300 years, that during that period suffering has decreased considerably, nor that people's chances of choosing their own styles of life have increased considerably" (1991b, 195). Rorty also argues that the increased restrictions are compensated for by a decrease in suffering and that democratic societies continue to have the best institutions for dealing with excessive restrictions on individual behavior—and that there are no concrete alternatives.

Here another point should be noted about where Rorty differs from many other major postmodern thinkers: he sees little political value in contemporary deconstructionist literary theory and in the project of overcoming Western metaphysical philosophy. In taking this position Rorty separates himself from Heidegger, Derrida, de Man, and many deconstructionist literary critics. The reason these thinkers take deconstruction seriously is that they believe that Western metaphysical philosophy (what Derrida calls "ontotheology") has a deep and terrible influence on everything else in Western culture.

This project comes from two claims in Heidegger's later philosophy. The first is that in striving to come up with a unique, closed, and final picture of the world, in searching for strong evidence and forceful arguments, Western metaphysical philosophy has identified truth with power, assuming that "truth is somehow a matter of the stronger overcoming the weaker" (Rorty 1991b, 32), as Rorty puts it. In other words, from the time of Plato, Western philosophy has been on a sick power trip, and at the end of the tradition, Nietzsche was still trying to do what Plato started out to do, which was to knock everyone down with his powerful picture of the world. The only difference between Nietzsche and Plato is that Nietzsche's "will to power" metaphysics made everything explicit. Heidegger's second claim is that, since philosophy is the substructure for everything else in Western culture, the West itself has been on a sick power trip. In Heidegger's view, Western science, modern technology and American pragmatism are all outgrowths of a power-hungry way of thinking—a way of thinking which a true "thinker" must constantly strive to overcome.

As Rorty tells the story, Derrida popularized these two claims in America, and they now lie behind the contemporary project of deconstruction. Rorty's response is that even if the tradition were on a power trip, and even if most of today's philosophers were still metaphysicians (which he denies), the claim that Western philosophy pervades and controls everything else in Western culture is "false" (1991b, 107). For Rorty it's absurd to think that metaphysical philosophy has that kind of cultural and political importance. Thus, while praising Derrida for his original deconstructions of past philosophers, Rorty sees these readings as having little value for today's political and moral struggles. As he says in response to de Man's claim that literary theory and critical-linguistic analysis are essential for political and moral progress:

> . . . it does not take any great analytic skills or any great philosophical self-consciousness to see what is going on. It does not, for example, take any "critical-linguistic analysis" to notice that millions of children in American ghettos grew up without hope while the U.S. government was preoccupied with making the rich richer— with assuring a greedy and selfish middle-class that it was the salt of the earth. Even economists, plumbers, insurance salesmen, and biochemists—people who have never read a text closely, much less deconstructed it—can recognize [that] the immiseration of much of Latin America is partially due to the deals struck between local plutocracies and North American banks and governments. (1991b, 135)

For Rorty, what the oppressed need isn't political reformers distracted by deconstructionist literary theory and the overthrow of Western metaphysical philosophy, but rather reformers who focus directly on concrete political problems and practical action. As he says in "Movements and Campaigns" (1995), what is needed isn't reformers distracted by sweeping intellectual "movements," but rather reformers who are engaged in specific political "campaigns." Instead of a reformer who prides himself on being a proper postmodern, standing far above the old-fashioned modernist, what is needed is a reformer who can create a significant job program for kids growing up in ghetto housing projects.

Here and throughout this section, we can see where Rorty differs from many other postmoderns: he is a pragmatist who believes that thought can only be justified in the realm of action, and, specifically, that it can only be justified by successful action in a democratic society. This pragmatism comes out in Rorty's criticisms of Marxism as well as in his criticisms of Foucault, Lyotard, Derrida, and the deconstructionists. It also comes out in his comparison of Dewey and Heidegger, two philosophers who have had a major influence on Rorty, and in the rest of this section, we will look briefly at what Rorty says about them.

To begin with, for Rorty, Dewey and Heidegger are, along with Wittgenstein, the most important Western philosophers, and Rorty praises both for their criticisms of metaphysical philosophy. But when he goes on to discuss their alternatives to metaphysics, he continues to praise only Dewey and has nothing good to say about Heidegger. Specifically, he praises Dewey's pragmatic alternative, which focused on social reconstruction in a democratic society, while he is highly critical of Heidegger's later philosophy, which was preoccupied with the search for Being.

Briefly, the "Being" that Heidegger searched for can be thought of as the ultimate truth about what lies behind, and gives form to, the way human beings think and act in the world; it is "that on the basis of which beings are already understood" (Dreyfus 1991, *xi*), and it includes a society's traditional patterns of behavior as well as its traditional language games and ways of describing the world. Although it gives form to a thinker's life and thought, it cannot be fully conceptualized, and therefore the thinker can become conscious of only a small part of it. Since, ultimately, it stretches back into darkness and mystery, the search for Being is endless, yet for Heidegger, it is the only topic worthy of thought in a postmetaphysical philosophy.

But for Rorty, Heidegger's search for Being is simply a distraction from the problems of human beings, and he sees it as marked off by the same kind of mysticism and "otherworldliness" which marked off Plato's metaphysical search for the "forms." At the end of "Overcoming the Tradition: Heidegger and Dewey," Rorty even concludes that "by offering us 'openness to Being' to replace 'philosophical argument' Heidegger helps preserve all that was worst in the tradition he hoped to overcome" (see Rorty 1982, 54). The point here isn't to determine whether Rorty is right about Heidegger's philosophy, but only to explain why he rejected it, and the reason is clear: for Rorty, it "has no general public utility" (1989, 118). The reason Rorty prefers Dewey's pragmatic alternative is also clear: he sees it as a philosophy which will help us in coping with the beings we encounter in a democratic society.

In defending Dewey over Heidegger, Rorty doesn't deny Heidegger's charge that Dewey's pragmatism is another expression of a will to power.

But whereas for Heidegger this just means more power sickness, for Rorty it means "an attempt to help achieve the greatest happiness of the greatest number by facilitating the replacement of language, customs, and institutions that impede that happiness" (1991b, 20). Unlike Heidegger, Rorty can see nothing inherently wrong with thought that attempts to control the world, and he claims that it is possible to "put power in the service of love . . ." (48), possible for politics to be "the appropriate vehicle for love . . ." (49). In taking this view Rorty also differs from Foucault, who, as we will see in a later chapter, assumes that the desire to control things is inevitably tied to dominance and oppression.

This brings us to a final difference between Rorty and Heidegger, a difference which also separates Rorty from many of Heidegger's postmodern followers: Rorty rejects their view of modern technology. According to this Heideggerian view, "modern technology" is much more than machine tools and practical know-how; it is also the culminating stage in the terrible will-to-power way of thinking about the world that began with Plato. As Heidegger says in "The Question Concerning Technology," modern technology is essentially an aggressive, pervasive and totalizing way of "revealing" (1977b, 12) the world, a way of revealing that leads us to see everything in nature, including human beings, as nothing but a resource, something to be used and then tossed away. Growing up under this way of revealing, we inevitably seek greater control, increased efficiency, and higher rates of production, and thus everything in our world, including ourselves, is reduced to a part of the stockpile or "standing reserve" (1977b, 17). With its great practical successes, this way of revealing the world is inherently expansive, and it is rapidly driving out other cultures and ways of revealing the world. It is thus producing a leveling down of "organized Uniformity" (1977b, 152), what Foucault calls the "normalization" of the world, and it should be thought of as a more centralized bureaucracy, increasing mass consumerism, and African villagers watching "Baywatch."

For Heidegger it should also be thought of as a way of revealing the world which closes us off to poetry, creative redescriptions, and the voice of the Other. In developing this claim Heidegger contrasts technological moderns with the "primordial" pre-Socratic Greeks; the latter, according to Heidegger, lived with a deep sense of the contingency of their way of life. In other words, they lived with a sense that there was nothing necessary about their traditional way of revealing or describing the world, and as a result, they also lived with an openness to alternatives, i.e., to poetry, creative redescriptions, and the voice of the Other. But for moderns, living under the spell of successful technological mastery, this sense of the contingency of our way of living in the world is lacking. And because we assume that there is something necessary about our descriptions of the world, we are deaf to poetry, redescription, and the beauty of what is Other.

Thus, despite the economic prosperity resulting from technological advances, Heidegger describes our era as "the darkening . . ." characterized by "the flight of the gods, the destruction of the earth, the transformation of men into a mass . . . [and] the hatred of everything free and creative" (1977a, 37–38). Or, as Rorty puts it, "for the Heideggerians technology is the Great Bad Thing in the world that is responsible for all contemporary evils," and it is what must be "overthrown" in order to produce a new and better kind of human being (1992).

As we will see in later chapters, this Heideggerian view of modern technology has exerted a major influence on postmodern thought, but for Rorty, the whole idea that we need to overthrow a single, all-encompassing way of revealing the world is nonsense. As he said in criticizing deconstructionist politics, reformers should instead attack the little things, e.g., specific cases of destructive technological development, and greedy, selfish, and cruel human beings. And in response to Heidegger's charge that modern technology has eliminated awareness of our contingency and deafened us to poetry and the voice of the Other, Rorty points out that along with the industrial revolution went romantic poetry, constant political and artistic revolution, and in the twentieth century a liberal culture that is hostile to ethnocentrism. In thinking about Rorty's response to the later Heidegger, and in particular about his refusal to separate philosophy from practical action, and technology from poetry and love of the Other, it is easy to accept Nancy Fraser's description of Rorty as a postmodern who is somewhere "between romanticism and technocracy" (see Malachowski 1990, 303)—and here again we can see what is special about a pragmatic brand of postmodernism.

Intellectual History and Metaphor as Mutation

Before concluding these two chapters on modern and postmodern philosophy, we should summarize Rorty's nonteleological view of the intellectual history of human beings—a view which is especially influenced by Darwin, Nietzsche, Wittgenstein, Hesse, and Davidson. To begin with, whereas modernists thought of intellectual history as primarily the history of changing thoughts about the world, for Rorty it is primarily the history of changing language—the history of changing vocabularies or descriptions of the world. And whereas modernists believe that, because of reason, the scientific method, or a closer inspection of the human soul, intellectual history is essentially the progression toward greater truth about the world, for Rorty there is no such progression. Instead, there are only changing redescriptions which make possible a new kind of intellectual and social life. The new descriptions replace the old simply because human beings find a use for them and not because they are more "accurate" than the old descriptions.

It isn't reason or truth which is at the root of this intellectual history; it's the imaginative use of old words in new ways. In other words, the intellectual history of the arts, of a sense of right and wrong, and of science is primarily "the history of metaphor" (1989, 16). In thinking of some key metaphors that have reshaped the history of Westerners, you might consider the early Christian redescription of God as "love," Luther's redescription of secular work as a holy "calling," and Newton's redescription of the regularities of nature as due to "gravity" (*gravitas*). In each case, an old word was used in a new way, and the consequence was a new kind of intellectual and social life. And once again Rorty emphasizes that there is nothing special about science and Newton's scientific revolution; here, too, the new way of thinking about the world follows the new use of an old word. In the beginning was always the metaphor.

In arguing that the major transitions in intellectual history are brought about by metaphor, Rorty follows Davidson in denying that when it is first used, a metaphor has cognitive content. In other words, when a speaker or writer first uses a word metaphorically, he is not attempting to convey a concept or meaning that already exists in his mind. Rather,

> tossing a metaphor into a conversation is like suddenly breaking off the conversation long enough to make a face, or pulling a photograph out of your pocket and displaying it, or pointing at a feature of the surroundings, or slapping your interlocutor's face, or kissing him. Tossing a metaphor into a text is like using italics, or illustrations, or odd punctuation or formats. (1989, 18)

The point here is that when an old word is first used in a new way, it is to produce an effect on a listener or reader and not to convey a concept. If the speaker or writer wanted to convey a concept, he would have spoken or written literally, using an expression that already had a meaning in the existing language.

In this view, when a word is first used metaphorically, it is a meaningless noise or mark. Since it doesn't have a place in the already existing language game, no one knows what it means, and it is not thought of as expressing something true or false. But after it has been used a few times and people begin to reflect on it in terms of their other beliefs and desires, a metaphorical sentence sometimes becomes meaningful. And when this happens, people change their beliefs and desires and start thinking about the world in a new way. If reflection does make sense of a metaphor, it becomes literalized, and its users then think it expresses something that is true or false. But again, we shouldn't think of a successful metaphor as a more accurate description of anything; instead, we should see it as a human creation which makes possible a new kind of intellectual and social life. For example, after God became "love," Romans no longer took their children to watch lions tear up human beings at the Colosseum.

Here it should be noted that although Rorty denies that, on first hearing, a metaphor has cognitive content, he does not deny that there are causes which explain why someone first uses an old word in a new way. The cause could be a kink in the brain or more likely a traumatic obsession in early childhood. For an example of the second possibility, Frank E. Manuel, in *A Portrait of Isaac Newton,* emphasizes that throughout much of Newton's childhood, he yearned for distant objects (his father died and went to Heaven before Newton was born, and when Newton was only three, his mother remarried and then lived away from him in his early years). Newton's later metaphorical use of *gravitas*—his claim that every body in the universe attracts and is attracted by other bodies—could thus be explained in terms of contingent childhood events. This doesn't explain Newton's mathematical ability, but it is interesting that Newton himself claimed that he arrived at his theory of gravity while sitting in his mother's garden.

Notice that in this view a metaphor is like a mutation—a novel form which is caused but is not the product of reason. In both cases, because of natural causes, something comes into the world but not as a result of reasoning. And in both cases, the new form sometimes endures for a time because of a particular environment that is receptive to it. With a succession of mutations, a new species is sometimes the result, and with a metaphor, a new kind of intellectual and social life is sometimes the result. It should also be emphasized that in both cases it is what follows the entrance of the new form into the world that is the key to its survival. If the savanna is receptive to a mutant who walks upright, the upright posture will replace the bent-over posture which preceded it, and if the intellectual and social world is receptive to the *gravitas* metaphor, it will replace the older description of the universe. It should also be emphasized that in neither case is anything being represented accurately; like a new species, a successful metaphor is simply a form that works in the world. And since the intellectual and social world is, like the natural world, constantly changing, we need to be alert to new and useful forms, alert to metaphors which can help us solve the old problems created by the old dead metaphors. We should also be alert to Rorty's main point about our intellectual history: "A sense of human history as the history of successive metaphors would let us see the poet, in the generic sense of the maker of new worlds, the shaper of new languages, as the vanguard of the species" (1989, 20).

An Insubstantial but Poetic Pageant

To conclude these last two chapters, if we give up on Descartes and Kant and take Rorty's postmodern turn, one thing is undeniable: everything that once was solid melts into thin air. Specifically, if we take this turn, we can no longer hang on to Descartes's certainty and Kant's rational and clear-cut moral rules. Nor can we hang on to our "true self," to our "natural feelings," or to the truth about the world. There are no foundations, and we will have to live with the thought that although we are clever animals, we do not have mirrors of nature in our heads. As teachers we will have to live with the thought that we are not passing on any eternal truths to our students.

On the other hand, none of this lack of solidity means nihilism. Nor does it mean that we should tell our students to stop reading or doing science, for both continue to be essential for solving some of our daily problems. We can also continue to praise scientists and other cultural heroes, but now they will be seen as people who are good at doing things, e.g., at healing, cleaning up the environment, teaching, redescribing, etc.—people who are good at solving problems and coping, but not people who have discovered truth.

What is gained is a freedom from what Nietzsche called a "burden"— the burden of thinking we have to find and live according to the truth, the burden of trying to force the world and its people into our rational categories, over and over again, without success. Without foundations or mirrors, what is solid has certainly melted into thin air, and what remains is obviously an insubstantial pageant, but at this point the linguistic imagination is no longer locked up in what Max Weber called "the iron cage" of reason and truth. Rather, it is freed to create a more imaginative play, perhaps with the same fantastic diversity that we find in Shakespeare.

3 From Modern to Postmodern Western Literature

> . . . the purpose of playing,
> whose end, both at the first and now, was and is to
> hold as 'twere the mirror up to Nature—. . . .
>
> — *Hamlet* (3.2.22–24)

> A novel is a mirror carried along a road.
>
> — Saint-Réal, as quoted by
> Stendhal (*The Red and the Black*,
> 78)

> "You have no use for the truth?" said Beatrice.
> "You know what the truth is?" said Karabekian. "It's some crazy
> thing my neighbor believes. If I want to make friends with him, I
> ask him what he believes. He tells me, and I say, 'Yea, yea—ain't it
> the truth.'"
>
> — Kurt Vonnegut (*Breakfast of
> Champions*, 209)

> A novel examines not reality but existence. And existence is not what
> has occurred; existence is the realm of human possibilities, every-
> thing that man can become, everything he's capable of. Novelists
> draw up *the map of existence* by discovering this or that human pos-
> sibility. But again, to exist means: "being-in-the-world." Thus *both*
> the character *and* his world must be understood as *possibilities*.
>
> — Milan Kundera (*The Art of the
> Novel*, 42)

A History of Modern Literature
from Racine to Woolf

It is often pointed out that, beginning in ancient Greece, Western writers
and artists were intent on representing reality in their literary and artistic works, and this goal continued to dominate Western literature and
art throughout the modern era. Just before the beginning of that era,
Shakespeare tells the playwright that he must above all "hold a mirror
up to nature," and while Shakespeare himself didn't consistently follow

this advice (thus his ghosts, witches, Ariel, and even entire fairy tale worlds, as in *A Midsummer Night's Dream*), the major modern writers who followed him did try to be consistent. The representations of these writers changed greatly from the seventeenth through the twentieth centuries, but the goal of holding a mirror up to nature did not—nor did the faith that it was somehow possible to mirror the world with language. For a superior discussion of the entire history of Western representation from Homer and the Old Testament to Virginia Woolf, see Erich Auerbach's *Mimesis*, which has greatly influenced the following discussion.

Phèdre *versus* Hamlet

As Auerbach shows, there was a major shift from Shakespeare's more relaxed attitude to a much stricter approach to representation during the later seventeenth century (1953, Chapters 13 and 15). The shift was influenced by several factors, but here the focus will be on the new faith in reason and the adoption of neoclassical aesthetics. Racine's *Phèdre* (1677) is perhaps the most famous play of the Age of Reason, and to illustrate how things changed during the early modern era it is convenient to compare it with *Hamlet* (1601), the most famous play of the Renaissance. Both works are tragedies, and thus show us what their audiences took seriously, and both are concerned with representing the world—but they "mirror" two different worlds.

To begin with, writing a few years after Descartes, Racine tries to show us the truth about a rational animal who lives in a rational universe, and in showing us this truth—about a nature which is written in the language of mathematics—Racine has no room for Shakespeare's imagination, wild metaphors, fantasy, or comedy. Nor does he have room for the lowly physical world which Shakespeare shows us in *Hamlet*—a world of cold nights, garbage, rotting corpses and worms, and where even tragic heroes get fat and grunt and sweat in a creatural way. In *Henry IV, Part 2*, Shakespeare makes fun of the classical idea that great heroes don't get tired and want a beer (Auerbach, 1953, 312), but Racine doesn't get the joke, and he has no room in his plays for the "low," physical side of human existence. His heroes are essentially rational minds, and they move through a lofty, spiritual world, elevated far above the lowly physical world. Phèdre does experience lust for her stepson, but it is a sublime passion and not the earthy kind of lust that Hamlet talks about when he tells Ophelia that it would "cost [her] a groaning" (*Hamlet*, 3.2.260) to satisfy him. In *Phèdre*, sexual activity is described as "ecstasy" and "reverie" (see Racine 1991).

Both Shakespeare and Racine show a class bias, and thus all of their tragic heroes are drawn from the nobility, but Shakespeare's less rational mirror shows us a great deal of the everyday, lower-class world. Specifically, in Shakespeare's play, everyday objects are described, and we learn something about the daily existence of soldiers on guard duty, traveling actors, and gravediggers. The kings who appear are also of the everyday sort, and they rule through devious policies and intrigue rather than through high moral values. None of this exists in Racine's rational mirror in *Phèdre*, which shows us only noble people with noble concerns. Phèdre's nurse appears, but only as a confidante, and we know nothing about the nurse's private existence and everyday concerns. Nor is Racine's king concerned with the daily activity of ruling, and, unlike Louis XIV, there is no suggestion that he maintains his power in the low, devious, normal way.

There is another major difference between the two mirrors: Shakespeare's characters are highly individualized, and Racine's are not. Not only does Hamlet have a particular physical nature which is flabby and out of shape, he also has an individualized past history, and his approach to the world is that of a unique human being. He has specific interests, views, and avocations, and we know that he is a university student and has a critical mind that thinks things through to the end. We also know that he is fast and clever with words and has a strange sense of humor and a twisted attitude toward women. On the other hand, we know very little about Phèdre, other than her past and thoughts only as they relate to the tragic action in which she is caught up. In a rationalist era that was preoccupied with the universal in human beings, it seems inevitable that playwrights would play down the individual and the idiosyncratic, and thus Racine is content to present a passionate "fallen woman" who, though noble and sublime in her great passion, has little individuality.

In summary, what appears in Racine's rational mirror isn't the physical, the everyday, the historical, or the particular; it is the spiritual, rational, and universal truth that Racine believes in, and as we can also see in the play, it is no joking matter. The play's style is in harmony with its early modern message that reason must dominate all aspects of human life, and that when it fails to do so—as when Phèdre gives in to her passion for her stepson—tragedy is the inevitable result. Here, too, we can contrast the two plays, for while Shakespeare does see the danger of being "passion's slave" (3.2.73), he also sees the danger of Hamlet's excessively rational approach to the world—the danger of "thinking too precisely on the event" (4.4.43), of practical action in the world coming to a standstill because "the native hue of resolution is sicklied o'er with the pale cast of thought" (3.1.92–93). Shakespeare, like his mentor Montaigne (especially in his essay "We Taste Nothing Pure" [see Montaigne, *Complete Works*]), could see the limits of a life devoted to reason, and thus Hamlet's tragedy, but at the beginning of the modern era, Racine shows no such ambivalence.

Despite the many differences in the two mirrors, Shakespeare and Racine agree on one crucial, modern point: human beings have a full and substantial self which is at the center of their thoughts, feelings, and actions. Like Descartes's "I" at the beginning of modern philosophy, both Hamlet and Phèdre have an essence which makes them what they are. They are human beings who stand outside of the world around them, and there is no suggestion that their thoughts and feelings have been shaped by external forces. Although at one point in *Phèdre* it is suggested that the heroine is a victim of fate, there is no suggestion that her thoughts and passions have their origins in a public language.

In concluding this discussion of the shift from Shakespeare's Renaissance plays to Racine's Age of Reason plays, it should be noted that while today's audiences find Racine's mirror of nature strikingly unrealistic, Racine's audience did not (Auerbach 1953, 388–89). Specifically, while we tend to think that too much is missing from Racine's representation of the world, his own audience felt that he had gotten beyond the insignificant trivia of daily life and thus was able to present the essential rational truth about the world. But as postmoderns like to point out, last year's "truth" about the world is this year's fantasy. Postmoderns will also emphasize something else about Racine's early modern tragedies: when the seventeenth century began worshiping reason, this led to an extremely narrow view of the world, a view which excluded not only the physical, the everyday, the historical, and the particular, but also what Foucault called "nonreason," i.e., madness, fantasy, and the imagination. What remains is a humorless, preachy, and static tragedy, a play that is so rationally pure that it seems comic to a postmodern sensibility.

Nineteenth-Century Romantic Literature

As Voltaire shows in *Candide*, during the second part of the eighteenth century, the faith in a rational nature became increasingly questionable, and by the beginning of the nineteenth century, there were two literary developments which reflect the declining faith: romanticism and the realist novel. In discussing the history of modern philosophy, we have already noted that although the romantics turned against the devotion to reason, they also shared a great deal with other modernists. This is also illustrated in romantic literature. Specifically, although the romantics turned against the neoclassical goal of holding an objective mirror up to nature, they did not turn against the idea that the poet should give us the truth. They differed from the neoclassicists only in assuming that it is subjective emotional truth which the artist must show us—the truth about our emotional life. And while they turned against the idea that we must be true to our rational nature, they did not turn against the idea that we have an essential nature to which we must be true—only now that nature is seen as an emotional nature. Thus Wordsworth speaks about "the universal heart" (Noyes 1956, 238), and he tells us that true poetry is "a spontaneous overflow of powerful feelings" (1967, 223) having its origins in reflection on emotions—emotions which are thought to be innate rather than the product of a particular community language. The romantic poet is seen as important not because he creates feelings, but because he puts the reader back in touch with those natural feelings which bind us into a united humanity.

On the other hand, the romantics challenged the neoclassical idea that the poet must strive to give us an objective copy of nature, and they also popularized the idea that the artist is a creator rather than a representer. Following Kant, they insisted that what is important about the poet isn't his rational ability to follow rules; it's his imagination—his imaginative metaphors and original descriptions of the world. But where Kant said that the poet must also give us a sense of a rational nature, and must therefore try to represent the world, the romantics began asserting that the artist should create a new world. This idea of the artist as creator will be found in Nietzsche a few years later, but without the contradictory romantic emphasis on art as the expression of "true feeling."

Nineteenth-Century Realist Literature

In his chapters "Hôtel de la Mole" and "Germinie Lacerteux," Auerbach discusses the realist tradition in the nineteenth-century novel. He points out that this tradition was initiated in France by Stendhal and Balzac in 1830. By this time, the French Revolution and the Napoleonic era had taken place, and Racine's rational universe was gone, but not his goal of representing the world. The difference is that now it is the everyday, historical world which must appear in the mirror. Thus, in *The Red and the Black,* Stendhal says that "the novel is a mirror carried along a road" (1961, 78)—a road on which flawed human beings are now chasing after money and social position rather than neoclassical honor. Since by 1830 the nonaristocratic classes were coming to power, the novel begins to take its heroes from those classes, and since human beings are now seen as wedded to their particular surroundings, the novel also begins to show how human lives are influenced by their surroundings.

Dickens, Thackeray, and George Eliot also write in this tradition, but as Auerbach points out, the attempt to give us an objective copy of the everyday, historical world is especially advanced in the second part of the nineteenth century by the French writers Flaubert and Zola. In the pursuit of such everyday, historical truth, Flaubert consistently tried to hide his own feelings and opinions about his characters, and in narrating their life histories he adopted a strict attitude of "objective seriousness" (Auerbach 1953, 490). What this means is that he tried to show us a character's world exactly as she would see it, if she could express herself accurately. For Flaubert, as for Racine, the writer's job wasn't to create a new world; it was to mirror the existing world. Specifically, it was to come up with the right words which would reveal the truth about a silly bourgeois dreamer like Emma Bovary.

In France, this realist tradition culminates in Zola's novels at the end of the nineteenth century, novels which, in their attempts to be "objective," are filled with lengthy environmental descriptions and endless concrete details. Zola believed that by turning himself into a scientist and doing scientific studies before writing his novels, he could create an objective language which mirrors exactly the world it describes—an objective language which would give us the truth, rather than just another imaginative description of the world.

With regard to the realists' picture of an individual human being, we have already mentioned that in their novels, the individual's fate is shown as greatly influenced by his historically determined environment. Thus Stendhal subtitles *The Red and the Black* "a chronicle of the nineteenth century" (1953, translator's note), and he shows that the fate of the main character, Julien Sorel, is determined by the historical conditions of the Restoration period in France. These conditions also determine the beliefs, concerns, and attitudes of the people around Sorel, and while the hero stands above them as a unique individual, by the time of Flaubert and Zola, all human beings are pictured as deeply submerged in a particular historically determined environment.

Yet even in these later realist novels there is still the sense that there is something "essentially human" which is repressed by environmental conditions. In other words, there is still the Rousseauean idea that the human self is deformed by—rather than created by—historical conditions and socialization. What is missing is the postmodern sense that there is nothing substantial that exists independently of socialization and an internalized collective language. This late modern way of thinking about human beings is especially obvious in the late-nineteenth-century novels of Tolstoy, and it can also be seen in Richard Wright's mid-twentieth-century realist autobiography, *Black Boy*. In this work, Wright emphasizes that a Jim Crow social environment had a major influence on the personality development of American blacks at the beginning of the twentieth century, but he also continues to think of a real self that exists independently of socialization and language. Thus, at the end of the book, after he has decided to leave the South and go north, he suggests that he will now have a chance to find his real self (1966, 284). A few years later, in *Invisible Man*, Ralph Ellison simply talks about "creating" himself; as he says, "Our task is that of making ourselves individuals" (1989, 354). And with the influence of existentialism in the 1950s and 1960s, the idea of a substantial, presocialized identity begins to disappear from Western literature. It is replaced by the paper-thin people who speak nothing but collective clichés, as in "the theater of the absurd" dramas of Beckett, Ionesco, Stoppard, and Albee.

The Stream of Consciousness Novel and To the Lighthouse

The movement toward a postmodern perspective is especially marked in the early-twentieth-century novels of James Joyce, Marcel Proust, and Virginia Woolf. Their novels differ from nineteenth-century realist novels in several ways (Auerbach 1953, 525–53). First, they give up on the attempt to give us an objective picture of a character's life history. Instead of trying to show us a life from beginning to end in all of its detail, they show us only a few of its random events, and even here there is no attempt to describe the events objectively. Rather, we see them through the eyes of a particular character, and we know the character only through a description of her "stream of consciousness." In other words, rather than attempt a complete, objective description of a character's true self, the author merely shows us a few of her changing impressions and ideas.

And in further retreat from the modernist attempt to give us an objective view of things, novelists like Joyce, Proust, and Woolf show us events and characters from several different points of view, as seen by different people at different times. What is especially important here is that none of the viewpoints is treated as privileged, as being more accurate or objective than the others. In Woolf's *To the Lighthouse*, for example, the question is posed—What is the main character, Mrs. Ramsay, really like?—and the "answer" is a lengthy description of her thoughts about a few changing events plus accounts of her given by several of the other characters at different times. Unlike Flaubert, the author doesn't have any privileged, objective information about a character. As Nietzsche said, "There are no facts, only interpretations" (Danto 1965, 76), and Woolf's novels remind us of the great gap between various subjective interpretations and the "original text." Flaubert also shows us events through the eyes of Emma Bovary, but thanks to his "objective" information about his character, the reader can clearly distinguish between Emma Bovary's stupid, romantic illusions and the reality of her lover. Because Woolf does not have such information, the reader of *To the Lighthouse* cannot make such a distinction, and by the end of the novel Mrs. Ramsay's personality still remains an enigma.

The realization that no one is privileged when it comes to truth and the shift to multiple interpretations or perspectives are extremely important to the development of postmodern thought, yet to some extent, *To the Lighthouse* falls within the modern truth-telling tradition. For in showing us a few random events in Mrs. Ramsay's life, such as her measuring a stocking, and in giving us a lengthy account of her thoughts in response to the event, and further, in showing us how she appears to many other characters on different occasions, there remains an attempt to give us a more objective view of her situation in the world. In other words, despite the author's awareness that we cannot get outside of how Mrs. Ramsay appears in human consciousness, there still remains the hope that the author can somehow reveal what Auerbach calls "a synthesized cosmic view or at least a challenge to the reader's will to interpretive synthesis" (1953, 549).

The idea here is that by focusing on a few contingent events in a human life, and by looking at those events through the eyes of many different people, we can somehow arrive at a more objective view of her. While agreeing that in order to live well in the world we need to focus on the contingent events in a human being's life, on the wealth of thought processes which they trigger, and on the way that they appear to different people at different times, a postmodern will also point out that there is no reason to think that such a focus will yield "a synthesized cosmic view" or anything else that can be called the "objective truth."

Postmodern Literature

As is suggested by this discussion of *To the Lighthouse*, it is a mistake to think that there are two clear-cut categories which can be classified "modern literature" and "postmodern literature." But during the past thirty years a distinctively postmodern culture has developed, and it has given rise to many books which, because of their themes and views of human existence, can be called "postmodern." In the rest of this chapter we will briefly discuss six works which can be so labeled: four novels, an autobiography, and a treatise on the novel.

Breakfast of Champions

It is convenient to begin with Kurt Vonnegut's *Breakfast of Champions*, a novel which puts down all of the basic modern beliefs, e.g., that we live in a rational universe; that human beings have a self that exists independently of language; that language represents reality; that reason, science, and technology are taking us to the Promised Land; and that a novelist should try to hold a mirror up to nature. But the book's main attack isn't on modernism, it's on American society during the Vietnam War—and it is this society which Vonnegut is attempting to overcome. *Breakfast of Champions* is thus a novel of social criticism, a postmodern novel that aims at social change.

The story is about the meeting of the two main characters, Dwayne Hoover, a successful but insane capitalist who lives in Midland City, Indiana, and Kilgore Trout, an unsuccessful but talented science fiction writer who lives in upstate New York. Before their meeting takes place we look at Dwayne's life, and we watch Trout hitchhike across the country en route to an "arts festival" in Midland. In the middle of the novel they meet in a Midland bar; Dwayne then reads one of Trout's novels, and because it is bad fiction, he beats up on several people, including his homosexual son, his mistress, and Trout (1973, 209–10). The novel ends as Dwayne is locked up, the arts festival is called off "because of madness" (284), and Trout starts home.

All of these events are clear, but the story is in the background for most of the novel. What is in the foreground is an entire society—specifically, a greedy and selfish capitalist society which is armed with dangerous technology, devoted to mindless consumption, and dominated by the mass media. It is also a society which is lonely and unhappy, and which has major ecological and social problems, including a polluted environment and massive alienation between the races, sexes, and classes. Finally, it is a society which is destroying not only Vietnam but also itself and—as its chemicals and pollutants spread out through the water, air, and earth—the entire planet. This extremely negative view of mainstream America is expressed on virtually *every page* of *Breakfast of Champions*, and like so many of us who were living through the Vietnam War, Vonnegut refused to balance things out with something positive. The result is a savage indictment of just about everything American, and the irony is that Americans quickly made this novel into a number-one bestseller.

But what is interesting from a postmodern point of view is Vonnegut's way of explaining America's problems. He begins with a preface which claims that Americans, like all human beings, are merely computers which do only what they have been programmed to do. There are also chemicals in these computer-beings, and, as we are told late in the novel, they also have "awareness," but they do not have a self that exists independent of their program. The program alone gives determinate shape to their thoughts, feelings, and behavior. Vonnegut also emphasizes that he is a machine like everybody else—specifically, a writing machine that prints out only what it has been programmed to print out. In other words, at the start of this postmodern novel, the author tells the reader that he will not be trying to express his self or represent the world accurately. Rather, we are told that the author will be doing nothing more than presenting his cultural program—the way he and other Americans have been taught to describe the world.

After this postmodern preface, the story begins with: "This is a tale of a meeting of two lonesome, skinny, fairly old white men on a planet which was dying fast" (1973, 7). The point isn't that Vonnegut and other Americans ought to begin their descriptions of human beings with a distinction between the races, but that this is how we have been programmed to think about human beings. As Vonnegut warns us in his preface, a great deal of our American program is terrible, "so this book is a sidewalk strewn with junk, trash which I throw over my shoulders . . ." (1973, 6). But as we soon see, Vonnegut is doing more than showing us our trashy American program; he is also showing us its consequences, and thus throughout *Breakfast of Champions,* the reader is constantly looking at a society which has a major racial problem. And not only is the reader confronted with a trashy program which defines women as "agreeing machines instead of thinking machines" (1973, 136), but he also sees the consequences—a society in which the women are subservient to men, no matter how stupid, cruel, or crazy the men are. To take one more example: there are many ads in the novel, and in them the program tells Americans to turn to products for pleasure rather than to people; the result, as we see throughout the novel, is a society which embraces products but not people—a society which is consequently lonely and unhappy. In this novel, the characters know the names of all the latest products, but they rarely remember the name of another human being unless he's a "one-armed albino" (104) or a "red-headed, Cockney midget" (105). Other than with their dogs and canaries, Vonnegut's product-filled consumers have few intimate relationships—although one of the novel's ads promises to solve the problem with a life-size rubber vagina!

America's social problems are thus explained as a consequence of the cultural program which Americans have internalized—a program which

Vonnegut calls "bad fiction." In locating the historical sources of this program, Vonnegut begins with the first Europeans—the "sea pirates"— who grabbed control of the continent and then passed on a culture which made color "everything" (11) and also encouraged grabbing as much wealth as possible, but did not encourage Americans to share with the less fortunate.

But this early history was only the beginning, and today's Americans are, above all, responding to a mass-media program, and Vonnegut insists that "most of the conversation in the country consist[s] of lines from television shows, both past and present" (236). Most of his characters show this influence by talking like a television program, e.g., simple vocabulary; clichés; short, undeveloped sentences; little analysis; lots of meaningless numbers; and a constant repetition of trivia. Like the writing machine which wrote this novel and repeats clichés, sentences, and even the entire first paragraph, the characters in *Breakfast of Champions* suffer from "echolalia." As Warhol was showing at the same time, endless repetition is the key to a mass-produced society.

Although Vonnegut's Americans are acting out a terrible media program, they are not aware of it. Only Kilgore Trout knows that he is "a character in a book by somebody who wants to write about somebody who suffers all the time" (241). And in writing this postmodern novel, Vonnegut's goal is to bring the reader to the same realization. In other words, he wants the reader to realize that his life is based on bad fiction rather than on truth. Vonnegut also knows what he is up against: the reader's modernist tendency to assume that his society's descriptions of the world are more than just "fiction," more than just another "story" that some human beings have dreamed up. If everybody in the most powerful nation in the world agrees with the media program—that a new BMW is what makes people happy—how could this description of things not correspond to reality? How could the program of an advanced, scientific society—and the millions of lives based on it—be the stuff that dreams are made on? Of course it's the truth. The main event in the novel—Dwayne's beating up on everybody after reading Trout's bad fiction and confusing it with reality—is based on the same confusion.

To wake us up, Vonnegut tells us that in *Breakfast of Champions* he has tried to avoid "old-fashioned" storytelling (209). This is because—with leading and minor characters, significant and insignificant details, and story lines that flow smoothly from beginning to middle to end—old-fashioned stories tell the reader that he is living in a rational world. To discourage such thought, throughout much of the novel Vonnegut deliberately focuses a great deal of attention on minor characters and insignificant details, and the narrative keeps jumping from time to time,

place to place, and character to character. At the close of the novel, "ETC."
replaces "the end" (295).

And whereas the traditional storyteller tries to create the illusion of
reality, Vonnegut wants his reader to realize that he is not making contact with anything but fiction. For this reason, Vonnegut constantly in-
terrupts the action with personal comments, e.g., "I do know who invented Kilgore Trout. I did" (32). Later, in bringing his story to a conclusion, the author tells us, "Let's see, let's see. Oh, yes—I have to explain a
jacket Trout will see at the hospital . . ." (249). The author also shows the
reader his childish drawings throughout the novel, and he even places
himself inside the story, so that we begin reading about a conversation
that the author is carrying on with one of his characters! With such in-
terruptions the illusory order of fiction is shattered, and the reader is
made to realize that what he takes to be reality is simply fiction—simply
another imaginative description of the world. What the reader sees is
that his thoughts and life are being controlled by a contingent symbolic
order that human beings have dreamed up, and not by anything rational or objective or true. He sees that he is involved in an insubstantial
pageant in which everything that seems solid just melts into thin air.
But he also sees that "symbols can be so beautiful, sometimes" (201), as
in Trout's imaginative science fiction stories, which are interspersed
throughout the novel. And finally, Vonnegut reminds us that the symbolic descriptions which we live under can be changed, and when they
are, so are we. The fly cannot get outside of the fly-bottle, but once she
becomes aware of it, she can change it and the life which is based upon
it. And sometimes she should change it, according to this postmodern
novel of social criticism.

The Autobiography of Malcolm X

Some of the ideas in *Breakfast of Champions* are also expressed in *The
Autobiography of Malcolm X*—a book which reflects the development of a
postmodern perspective not only on an individual's life history, but also
on power and race relations. This development is clear if Malcolm's
autobiography is compared with Richard Wright's autobiography, *Black
Boy*, which was published twenty-one years earlier. Both books are concerned with power, race relations, and the personality development of
American blacks, and both books want to change things, but the perspective is different.

In *Black Boy*, Wright tries to show that in the Jim Crow South, whites
maintained their power over blacks through social institutions, and in
particular, he tries to show that both white and black thought and behavior are controlled by "traditional racial roles" (1966, 93) that can be

traced back to slavery. What Wright emphasizes is that as black children grew up they were expected to play the role of a "black boy"—specifically, of an ignorant, dependent, and happy-go-lucky child who would never grow up—and that this role was supported by a system of automatic rewards and punishments. What Wright also shows is that as a result of a lifetime of playing this role and watching other blacks play it, many were "not conscious of living a special, separate, stunted way of life" (216). If Wright is correct, the inferior role began to seem natural, and it defined how the players thought about themselves. Thus, like other traditional realists, Wright emphasizes the shaping power of social institutions. But he has nothing to say about the shaping power of a collective public language, and even at the end of *Black Boy*, when he discovers that words are "weapons" (272), he never concludes that they are his main enemy—that language itself was the main shaping force behind the Jim Crow way of life that he was fighting.

Malcolm is also concerned with personality development and power relations between whites and blacks in his *Autobiography*, but in this book, language is in the foreground. What Malcolm emphasizes is what the French postmodern historian, Foucault, was beginning to emphasize at the same time: that power relations are mediated and shaped by language—more specifically, by the prevailing cultural descriptions of groups and what they should do in the world. Such descriptions are found not only in everyday discourse, but also in movies, on television, and in textbooks.

With regard to personality development, both Malcolm and Foucault were beginning to see the postmodern point that is being emphasized throughout this book: that individual human beings don't first categorize and make value judgments about themselves and the groups they belong to, and then later express those categories and judgments in language. Rather, it's the other way around, with the categories and judgments coming last. As Foucault reminds us, the homosexual child doesn't first discover his homosexuality, and then interpret what it means; he finds it already interpreted for him by the way his society describes it. Nor does a child start interpreting his skin color and the "race" he "belongs to" before he learns a society's language and how it describes light and dark skin and racial groups. Since the child's eyes reveal a continuum of color from very dark to very pale, right from the start his mental separation of "the whites" from "the blacks" is made under the guidance of linguistic categories, and as John Edgar Wideman has said, "The separation of white *from* black is preparation for white *over* black" (1994, 79). It was this second idea which Malcolm X was fighting, and he constantly emphasized that a racist language controls the thinking and

personality development of American whites and blacks. Thus, in trying to rehabilitate drug addicts and disorganized and apathetic ghetto
personalities, he focused directly on the language that shaped those personalities.

Notice the postmodern way of thinking about oppression and power:
Malcolm knew that he wasn't *just* fighting the racist white man, and he
knew he wasn't *just* fighting the thinking that existed in ghetto minds;
what he understood was that he was also fighting a traditional public
language that came between the two and shaped both. Specifically, he
understood that behind his white teacher, who told him that black people
become carpenters and not lawyers (1964, 36), and also behind the black
high school dropout, there was something else—traditional American
descriptions that center on white people as "minds" and black people
as "bodies." From this postmodern perspective, language becomes our
chief "enemy":

> The American press made the murderers look like saints and the
> victims like criminals. They made criminals look like victims and
> indeed the devil look like an angel and angels like the devil. (1991,
> 37)

As Rorty once put it while talking to a group of high school students:
"The oppressed must always realize that they are fighting the way previous generations have described things."

In dealing with this postmodern "enemy," neither Malcolm nor the
Black Muslims stopped with analysis; they didn't just tell disorganized
ghetto blacks, "You're a victim of the white man's brainwashing." They
also systematically tried to create a new language, a new way of describing the world that would create self-pride and determination in
place of self-hate, apathy, and intellectual laziness. Thus, instead of "the
so-called Negro," the black man is redescribed not as a descendant of
slaves, but of the "strong black tribe of Shabazz" (1964, 164), not from
the Africa of cannibals, but from the place of "glorious civilizations"
(1991, 142). The color of this original man is also "beautiful," the color of
God. Whites, on the other hand, are redescribed as "bleached-out" (1964,
165), "pale-skinned, cold-blue-eyed devils" (166), and they were created
not by God but by a dissatisfied black scientist who rebelled against
Allah. Finally, although at present the whites have the power, they are
on borrowed time, and, by Allah's Will, they will soon lose out to the
morally superior people of color. (For a classic short story which also
reverses the traditional white-over-black symbolism but without the
racism, see Alice Walker's "The Diary of an African Nun." Here, through
the eyes of an African woman who has become a nun, "white" becomes

the "icy whiteness" of snow, and it is associated with an icy European religion which worships a virgin God and has "stifled passion," in contrast to the "rich" and "hot black soil" of Africa, where people have passionately worshipped resurrection in *this* world—a story which could have been written by one of the "discontents" in Freud's *Civilization and Its Discontents.*")

The goal of this kind of rhetoric, and also of the Muslims' strict ascetic code, is to overcome the deep sense of inferiority and apathy found in so many people in the ghetto and to turn them toward more disciplined and productive lives. In other words, the goal is rebirth through redescription, which can also be seen as the main theme in Malcolm X's *Autobiography*. This theme is especially illustrated in the life of Malcolm: in the first part of the book we see him as an amoral hustler, the product of street language which defines an honest worker as a "slave" (1964, 44), but after redescribing himself in prison, we watch Malcolm's transformation into a responsible, disciplined black leader.

In conclusion, it should be pointed out that despite its postmodern focus on the shaping power of language and rebirth through redescription, Malcolm X's *Autobiography* is not fully postmodern. What especially keeps it in the modern tradition is the assumption that, once the slave master's language is thrown out, the True, African Self will appear. From a postmodern point of view, this is a myth. To begin with, there is no reason to believe that any self exists independently of a particular language; and even if one did, it would not appear in consciousness. Nor can it be found through "getting in touch with one's roots." In short, nothing will appear in consciousness with the removal of the master's language except another language, another way of describing the self. X is our permanent condition as human beings, and our greatness lies not in our ability to find ourselves, but in our ability to recreate ourselves through redescription. This kind of greatness is classically illustrated in Malcolm X's *Autobiography*.

The Painted Bird

Jerzy Kosinski's *The Painted Bird* is a postmodern novel that deals with the problem of the Other. Since the theme of the Other is at the center of postmodern moral thought, and since Kosinski's treatment of it takes us to the roots of the problem, this novel requires a fuller treatment than the other works discussed in this section.

The story takes place in Eastern Europe against the background of Nazi occupation during the Second World War, and it is about what happens to a small boy who has been sent for safety's sake from his urban home to stay with an old peasant villager until the war is over. The old woman dies shortly after his arrival, and in the rest of the novel we watch a stray child, thought to be a Jew or a gypsy, wander from village to village in search of food, shelter, and protection. What we see is that although he is harmless, most of the villagers brutally abuse him. Only a few will take him in, and when he does get close to the rest, they usually utter magic spells to ward off an evil spirit, assault him, or try to drive him away. Several times he is almost killed. The story ends when the boy is reunited with his parents at the end of the war; he survives, but he is also deeply scarred by his experiences.

It is thus a story which focuses attention on an innocent human being who is kicked around by other human beings. In reading it, we are forced to meditate on why this happens in human societies—on the social and psychological factors which might explain why a harmless boy is mistreated by a group of villagers. Kosinski gives us part of the answer in a brief preface when he tells us that the boy differs from the villagers in two basic ways: he is dark, while they are fair, and he speaks the educated dialect of the city, while they speak the uneducated dialect of the countryside. This theme of difference runs throughout the novel, but the more complete explanation of the boy's mistreatment is provided in Chapter 4. In this chapter he has managed to find shelter with a villager named Lekh, a bird-trapper who lives in the forest. Lekh has a passionate love affair with Ludmila, an unbalanced peasant woman, and in the following crucial passage, Kosinski describes what happens when she hasn't returned for several days:

> Sometimes days passed and Stupid Ludmila did not appear in the forest. Lekh would become possessed by a silent rage. He would stare solemnly at the birds in the cages, mumbling something to himself. Finally, after prolonged scrutiny, he would choose the strongest bird, tie it to his wrist, and prepare stinking paints of different colors which he mixed together from the most varied components. When the colors satisfied him, Lekh would turn the bird over and paint its wings, beak, and breast in rainbow hues until it became more dappled and vivid than a bouquet of wildflowers.
>
> Then we would go into the thick of the forest. There Lekh took out the painted bird and ordered me to hold it in my hand and squeeze it lightly. The bird would begin to twitter and attract a flock of the same species which would fly nervously over our heads. Our prisoner, hearing them, strained toward them, warbling more loudly, its little heart, locked in its freshly painted breast, beating violently.
>
> When a sufficient number of birds gathered above our heads, Lekh would give me a sign to release the prisoner. It would soar, happy and free, a spot of rainbow against the backdrop of clouds,

and then plunge into the waiting brown flock. For an instant, the birds were confounded. The painted bird circled from one end of the flock to the other, vainly trying to convince its kin that it was one of them. But, dazzled by its brilliant colors, they flew around it unconvinced. The painted bird would be forced farther and farther away as it zealously tried to enter the ranks of the flock. We saw soon afterward how one bird after another would peel off in a fierce attack. Shortly, the many-hued shape lost its place in the sky and dropped to the ground. When we finally found the painted bird it was usually dead. Lekh keenly examined the number of blows which the bird had received. Blood seeped through its colored wings, diluting the paint and soiling Lekh's hands.

Stupid Ludmila did not return. Lekh, sulking and glum, removed one bird after another from the cages, painted them in still gaudier colors, and released them into the air to be killed by their kin. One day he trapped a large raven, whose wings he painted red, the breast green, and the tail blue. When a flock of ravens appeared over our hut, Lekh freed the painted bird. As soon as it joined the flock a desperate battle began. The changeling was attacked from all sides. Black, red, green, blue feathers began to drop at our feet. The ravens flew amuck in the skies, and suddenly the painted raven plummeted to the fresh-plowed soil. It was still alive, opening its beak and vainly trying to move its wings. Its eyes had been pecked out, and fresh blood streamed over its painted feathers. It made yet another attempt to flutter up from the sticky earth, but its strength was gone. (1978, 49–51)

The "painted bird" is the Other, and it's clear that, as the painted bird is to the flock, so the boy is to the villagers. The action is also clear: when the painted bird tries to enter the ranks of the flock, the flock's first reaction is confusion, and then attack. As the flock sees it, safety lies in similarity, danger in difference, and the attack is thus a fear reaction to drive away danger. Such behavior is probably normal for all "herd animals" (i.e., social animals which depend on a social group for survival), and the mainly unconscious thought processes involved might be summed up as follows: "Since the group that looks and talks like me helps me to survive, it is safe, good, and so are people who resemble us; and (through simple either/or reasoning), whoever is different is dangerous, bad." As Sartre says, "To the Normal Man, to be different and to be wrong are one and the same" (1963, 24). And as Kosinski puts it in explaining why thoughts of evil enter our minds when it gets dark: "far beyond the boundaries of the known the Devil sits . . ." (1978, 59).

These associations probably provide the common starting point for most thinking about the Other, but a fear of what is different is not the whole story, at least not for human beings. For what we see in this painted bird passage is that a human being will *make* an animal different from its own kind, even when it is not. In other words, human beings not only fear the Other, they also have a need to have an Other in their lives. And it is this need which explains why the Other always seems to be in our thoughts, why our societies are designed to make some people different, and why reason and education have not eliminated the problem.

In exploring the roots of this need, Kosinski shows us that the presence of the Other is tied to several perennial human problems. First, there is the problem of establishing a unified social group. It is always a problem to bring individual human beings together, and the peasants in *The Painted Bird* are normally at each other's throat—except when the boy comes up the road. At that point, they are united by the thought that they are combating the evil Other. In *The Eumenides*, Aeschylus even claimed that "unanimous hatred is the greatest medicine for a human community" (Burkert, Girard, and Smith 1987, 126), and this need for group unity helps to explain a statement that is often attributed to Hitler: "If the Jew didn't exist, we'd have to invent him."

Kosinski also shows us that the Other solves another perennial human problem: the problem of evil. This problem arises because the villagers, like human beings everywhere, have violent and lustful thoughts and do things which violate the moral code that they are supposed to follow. Thus, while wanting to be good, they are aware of evil. When the boy comes up the road, the problem is solved through projection: by "painting" him evil, they remain good. Here we can see that their physical cruelty is not simply an attempt to keep the boy at a safe distance; it is also an attempt to destroy the evil which they have projected into him. At this point we can see why the boy can only be driven a safe distance away, rather than killed; for without the presence of the Other, the evil within would have to be faced.

For Kosinski, the projection of evil is fundamental in explaining our relationship with the Other, but he also shows us that with this projection, the Other comes to hold exciting parts of our secret self, and so there is ambivalence. Thus, upon finding discarded pictures of Jews from concentration camp trains, the peasants collect them and use them while masturbating and even put them on the walls of their Christian homes. (Richard Wright [1965] also saw this side of the problem in American racism, and in the opening scene of "Big Boy Leaves Home," a Jim Crow white lady accidentally comes upon some naked black teenagers at their swimming hole; then, despite her hysterical fear of the unknown black body, she is strangely paralyzed and unable to walk away. At the end of the story this leads to a terrible lynching that is also a sex party.)

Despite the ambivalence, there can be no doubt about where the evil is. For the villagers it is "proved" not only by the boy's otherness, but also by the fact that he and his kind are the people who are getting bashed around in God's universe. Since God is good and His universe is just, if millions of Jews are being exterminated in concentration camps, they *must* be guilty. God, the villagers reason, is simply punishing the Jews for their ancestors' crime of killing Jesus two thousand years earlier. Such comforting "blame-the-victim" reasoning seems needed if the villagers are to keep their faith that the universe is good and that justice is in God's hands. The alternative is to accept a chaotic universe and that human beings are responsible for whatever justice or injustice there is in the world.

Kosinski also shows the reader that the Other helps to solve another human problem: the desire to rise up and live a significant life in a universe in which we seem to be small and insignificant. For the peasants, who are poor and cannot stand up to the Nazi invaders, the problem of achieving status and significance is particularly painful—until the boy comes up the road. At that point it becomes possible for them to look down on someone else, and by treating him as an inferior being, they affirm at the same time that they are superior. Then, when they set out to minimize his evil influence in the world, their lives take on great significance. Here we might also think of the very average human beings who have joined the Klan and who have patrolled the California border, trying to stop the "brown hordes" from contaminating American society. Here we can also see why we so often find the Other—whether of another race, religion, sex, nationality, occupation, personality type, or whatever—in our thoughts; why it is so easy to pass from thoughts of "us" to thoughts of "them." And in the most vicious images in this novel we see human beings trying to get to the top by cutting down other human beings.

To return to the key passage, we can see that there is something more general behind Lekh's willingness to persecute a painted bird. He is frustrated because his girlfriend hasn't returned, and, as is normally the case, frustration leads to rage and aggression. Frustration isn't the only cause of aggression, but it is a major cause. The problem is to find a target, for early in life we are exposed to moral codes which make us feel guilty about taking it out on "our own kind." The Other provides the moral loophole, and here we can see why Lekh must paint the bird: only when the victim is seen as Other can there be aggression without guilt. In normal times the aggression that follows frustration is usually expressed verbally, with humiliating and cutting remarks, but when there is extreme frustration the aggression gets more brutal. This in turn calls for more extreme "painting" to justify the increased brutality. And here we should keep in mind that the Third Reich took shape during the frustrating Great Depression, which made a whole nation feel small and insignificant.

In one of the chapters we see a villager raping a Jewish girl, and we also see that he cannot withdraw. Since to some extent frustration, the need for group unity, and thoughts of evil and insignificance are always with us, the real question raised by *The Painted Bird* is whether human existence is possible without the Other—whether we *can* withdraw. There was a time when many Western intellectuals thought that communism was the answer, but, as Kosinski shows in a chapter on the Soviet communists, this is a false hope. What he makes clear is that although they treat the boy exceptionally well, their social order is also based on the persecution of the Other—that within communist societies there has been a constant persecution of the "enemies of communism." As other postmoderns have sadly pointed out, despite different economic arrangements, the problem of the Other has remained at the center of communist society in China as well as Russia.

Before discussing Kosinski's postmodern style, we should focus on the second question which the novel asks the reader to meditate on: What happens to human beings who are constantly treated as the Other? As we follow the boy's wanderings from village to village, the answer is clear: he changes from being confident, relaxed, and harmless to being negative, defensive, and violent. His innocent six-year-old way of looking at the world in the first chapter is soon forgotten, and before long he literally loses his voice—in other words, his old way of describing the world. What happens psychologically is that he begins "identifying with the aggressor," and as a result he begins to idealize the strong while hating weak people like himself. In one scene he even pictures a brutal but powerful SS officer as God, while he sees himself as a "squashed caterpillar oozing in the dust" (1978, 117–20). As postmoderns stress, human thought about the world is intimately tied to power, and in *The Painted Bird* Kosinski shows us that when human beings feel powerless, they inevitably hate themselves. After a few years of being a powerless Other, when he almost dies this innocent boy is sure he is going to hell.

Only after the boy's reunion with his parents at the end of the novel does he regain his voice. But when he does, we see another example of Nietzschean self-overcoming-through-redescription. Specifically, after regaining his voice, Kosinski is able to write this semi-autobiographical novel, and in it we do not see a squashed caterpillar, but an innocent "painted bird" who is the sacrificial victim of a brutal but normal group of "bird-painters." What Kosinski accomplishes in *The Painted Bird* is what is accomplished in the Gospels: a redescription that shows the Other as innocent and the majority as wrong.

As an example of postmodern fiction, in this novel Kosinski makes no attempt to hold a realistic mirror up to nature. Thus there is no attempt to provide an objective description of the villagers and their world, and the reader is given only a few general comments about the time and place of the story. Nor does Kosinski tell us how the boy manages to get away from some villages or how he ends up in others, and at the end of the novel we still don't know the boy's name. The novel's images—of savage violence, mutilated eyeballs, the boy being thrown into a pool of filth—are brutally concrete, but they are not designed to give us an objective picture of the world. Nor has Kosinski attempted to write a psychological novel; he tells us about the boy's changing self-image and about some of his dreams, but there is no attempt to give us a full and complete description of the boy's psyche.

Instead of providing us with social or psychological realism, the novel—specifically, its descriptions of the environment, its stark images, its many animal fables, and a sequence of events obviously meant to illustrate the central theme—is designed to focus our attention on a single aspect of human existence: the relation of social groups to the Other. In taking this approach to the novel, in which one aspect of existence is presented in isolation from everything else, Kosinski is certainly open to the charge of "distortion," especially by moderns who believe in the possibility of an "objective picture of the world." No doubt many critics will level the same charge against Kosinski's "one-sided" treatment of his theme. But few readers would deny that in *The Painted Bird* Kosinski has managed to transform the twentieth-century nightmare into an unforgettable novel, and it is difficult to think of a better starting point for meditating on the moral problem of the Other.

Being There

Postmodern thought has been greatly influenced by an increasing awareness of the importance of revolutions in communications technology—especially the writing revolution, which will be discussed briefly in the last chapter, and the video revolution, which will be discussed here. What has been emphasized is that these revolutions in communications technology have changed not only the way human beings communicate, but also the way they think and live in the world, as did the first major communications revolution, when human beings invented language. In *Being There* the focus is directly on the impact of television, and the reader is asked to think about what it means to exist in a video-dominated world.

Whereas it is the eye of the Other which dominates the action in *The Painted Bird*, it is the eye of television which dominates *Being There*.

The main character, Chance, is a retarded, middle-aged gardener who has spent his entire life on a rich man's estate and has had few interactions with other human beings. He has been influenced by his work in the garden, but his identity and knowledge about the world are taken mainly from the television set that he spends his life watching. At the end of the first chapter he is told that the rich man has died and that he will have to leave the estate, and during the rest of the novel, we see how he makes out in the modern world. We also see how, after appearing on television through a series of accidents, a retarded gardener with only a television education could be seriously considered as a candidate for public office, as vice president of the United States!

In making the story plausible, Kosinski develops two interrelated themes: the nature of televised pictures of the world, and the influence of television watching on personality development. In focusing on the first theme, Kosinski shows us that, contrary to the claims of the first ads for television, a televised picture of the world is not like "being there." He also stresses that instead of thinking of television as representing the world, we should think of it as creating a world—a new kind of world that differs greatly from the world which writing and print created. As Kosinski says at the start of the novel:

> The set created its own light, its own color, its own time. It did not follow the law of gravity that forever bent all plants downward. Everything on TV was tangled and mixed and yet smoothed out: night and day, big and small, tough and brittle, soft and rough, hot and cold, far and near. (1970, 5)

Both points—that television is creating its own world, and that it is a world in which everything is "smoothed out," i.e., in which differences are reduced and eliminated, so that everything seems like everything else—are illustrated in the novel. In addition to the differences mentioned above, it is often pointed out that television seems to be eliminating the distinction between "fictional" events and "real" events, and this, too, is illustrated in the novel. When Chance is asked what he thinks about the Vietnam War, he responds: "The war? Which war? I've seen many wars on TV," and a woman next to him concludes:

> Alas, . . . in this country, when we dream of reality, television wakes us. To millions, the war, I suppose, is just another TV program. But out there at the front, real men are giving their lives. (89)

It is difficult to believe that the situation was different during "Desert Storm." And who could distinguish between "entertainment" and "news" while watching the chase, arrest, and trial of O. J. Simpson?

If Kosinski is right, televised pictures of the world are also eliminating the distinction between intelligent and stupid human beings. To see why, we are asked to think about how Chance appears on television, as opposed to how he would appear if he were actually in our living room. In the latter situation we would interact with him personally and watch how he responds to our questions, and thus we would quickly see that he is not very bright. But, as is illustrated when Chance appears on the "This Evening" talk show, the situation is different on television. The main reason is that television "reflect[s] only people's surfaces," and thus "his thinking could not be televised" (54). The camera can show Chance's image (and as a blend of television personalities and good looks, Chance's image is particularly appealing), but it cannot show us his inner thought processes. Thus it is often pointed out that when we watch a politician on television, we are more likely to think about his personality—is he good-looking, natural, lying, warm, strong?—than about his reasoning powers.

The fact that people talk on television shows doesn't add much to what the camera tells us about their intelligence. This is partially because speeches are ghosted and everything is carefully staged. But the deeper problem is that what *all* people say on television is controlled by the demands of a public communications medium which is aimed at pleasing a mass audience. As the postmodern sociologist Baudrillard says, "the mass(age) is the message." In other words, television must above all entertain and massage a mass audience, and for this reason it cannot afford much talk which is complicated and difficult to follow. Nor can it afford many sentiments and beliefs which challenge the norm. And when the Other does appear on talk shows, notice how its voice is constantly surrounded by the host and audience, both reassuring us that our prevailing sentiments and beliefs are the only correct ones. In general, what the mass(age) medium demands is television personalities and political candidates who stick to the simple, clichéd, and socially approved surface.

This mass(age) way of talking is strengthened by something else which Kosinski emphasizes about television communication: the fact that the television talker cannot see his audience—cannot see what impressions his words are making on the faceless millions who are watching him. In such a situation it seems best to play it safe, to avoid anything too private or complicated, in favor of collective descriptions and sentiments which will not offend and which everyone can follow. In the metaphor which dominates *Being There*, what television demands is a kind of reassuring "blankness."

Given such a communication situation, even in dealing with complicated issues, television invites simple-minded comparisons instead of complicated reasoning. Thus Chance seems quite normal when, in response to the question of why the economy is declining, he says:

> In a garden . . . growth has its season. There are spring and summer, but there are also fall and winter. And then spring and summer again. As long as the roots are not severed, all is well and all will be well. (54)

Such reassuring but blank responses are made for mass(age) television politics, and thus on "Meet the Press," a White House economic advisor responded to a question from a CNN interviewer about an economic recession by saying:

> I don't think it's the end of the world even if we have a recession. We'll pull back out of it again. No big deal. . . . Things change. The tide comes in, it comes out. The moon goes up, it comes down.[1]

But what makes Chance a particularly suitable candidate in an era of televised politics is that his personality has been formed by television, and here we should turn to Kosinski's ideas about the relation between television watching and personality development. The main issue is the kind of personality which is formed from interacting with a television set rather than interacting with other human beings. To begin with, Kosinski argues that if a child's sense of well-being comes from flicking channels rather than from acting in the world, he will develop a passive personality and also one that is naive about the difficulty of bending the real world his way. The naive optimism is encouraged not only by the TV watcher's ability to change the world with a mere flick of the channel changer, but also by television's quick and simple solutions at the end of the half-hour show. Kosinski also emphasizes that a human being who grows up in front of her TV set will lack a strong sense of herself as an individual human being, for such a sense can be developed only through acting in the world and then observing how other human beings respond to one's actions. As Kosinski says:

> By looking at him, others could make him be clear, could open him up and unfold him; not to be seen was to blur, to fade out. Perhaps he was missing a lot by simply watching others on TV and not being watched by them. (12)

Here Kosinski is assuming the postmodern point that an eye turned inward cannot see a distinct self; he is also following Sartre in assuming that an individual's sense of self must therefore depend on the eye of the Other, i.e., on how other human beings see and label him. But the eye of the television set doesn't look back at the watcher, and since it doesn't—since it doesn't say you're smart or dumb, brave or cowardly, creative or a bore, good or bad—a child who spends a lot of time interacting with his television set will have a poorly developed sense of himself. Finally, the development of a blank personality will also be encouraged through the watcher's identification with the personalities he sees on TV; since they express only safe and clichéd emotions and thoughts, he, too, will develop a safe and clichéd personality.

Since print reflects thought processes and takes the reader into a more private world, reading would work against the formation of a clichéd, channel-changing personality, yet, as so many channel-changing students say, reading is "boring" compared to a TV massage. But the final result is a human being with no more personal identity than a "blank page." While such an identity adds to Chance's political appeal in a democratic society (since it enables people from diverse backgrounds to project into him what they want to see), Kosinski does not suggest that it is good for a democratic society.

Notice that in presenting this meditation on how television is influencing human life, Kosinski begins with two major postmodern propositions: first, we should think of language as creating rather than representing the world. What Kosinski adds is that the mass(age) language of television is creating a new kind of human world, a world in which differences and distinctions are being eliminated. The second proposition is that the self isn't expressed by language; it is created by language. In other words, the self is an extension of language, rather than the reverse. Today we are simply becoming extensions of television language (this point is made dramatically in David Cronenberg's 1982 postmodern film *Videodrome*, which shows a pulsating videocassette being shoved directly into the main character's guts). But what Kosinski adds is that the language of television differs from written language, and thus a new kind of self is being created. Unlike the earlier self, the new one will be "smoothed out" and shaped like a cliché, with little uniqueness, a lack of self-awareness, unable to distinguish between reality and make-believe or intelligence and stupidity. Kosinski calls it a "videot!"

The Art of the Novel *and* The Unbearable Lightness of Being

In *The Art of the Novel* the Czech novelist Milan Kundera has given us a postmodern view of the novel as an art form, and in *The Unbearable Lightness of Being,* he has written one of the most interesting postmodern novels. Kundera is important because he shows us not only the possibilities for a postmodern novel, but also for a postmodern way of living in the world.

In *The Art of the Novel* he discusses the history of the Western novel, beginning with a contrast between Cervantes and scientific thinkers such as Galileo and Descartes. The contrast: while the new Western scientists were anxiously striving to capture the truth about the world, the novelists were saying that human beings live in a relative, ambiguous world in which there is no truth. In developing this theme, Kundera especially praises the novels of Rabelais, Cervantes, Sterne, Diderot, Balzac, Stendhal, Flaubert, Dostoevsky, Tolstoy, Proust, Joyce, Kafka, and Broch, and he concludes with the Jewish proverb "Man thinks, God laughs." In other words, these novelists remind us that God laughs at the sight of man thinking:

> Because man thinks and the truth escapes him. Because the more men think, the more one man's thought diverges from another's. And finally, because man is never what he thinks he is. (1986, 158)

For Kundera, the novel is thus an "echo of God's laughter" (158). It is also the enemy of the man who hasn't heard of God's laughter, the man who thinks he lives in truth, and especially the totalitarian. As Kundera says:

> The world of one single Truth and the relative, ambiguous world of the novel are molded of entirely different substances. Totalitarian Truth excludes relativity, doubt, questioning; it can never accommodate what I would call *the spirit of the novel*. (14)

As to the value of an art form that echoes God's laughter at our pretensions to truth, Kundera concludes:

> But it is precisely in losing the certainty of truth and the unanimous agreement of others that man becomes an individual. The novel is an imaginary paradise of individuals. It is the territory where no one possesses the truth, neither Anna nor Karenin, but where everyone has the right to be understood, both Anna and Karenin. (159)

Thus, while Totalitarian Truth is threatened by the novel, democracy thrives on it. For the novel's questioning and doubting, with its multiplicity of characters and points of view, remind us that no one knows the truth, including the totalitarian who wants to impose his order on the rest of us. Such a reminder breeds tolerance and curiosity about the Other, helping to create a democratic "paradise of individuals." Here it should be noted that when the Russians invaded Czechoslovakia in 1968, Kundera's novels were banned from the public libraries in the name of Communist Truth.

In discussing the novel as an art form, Kundera develops another major theme: that the novel is above all the art form which raises questions about our existence in the world as self-conscious beings. Thus the novel also explores the mystery of the self, but its main focus is not on an encapsulated, essential self, but rather on human existence in the world. As Kundera says, the novel is "the great prose form in which an author thoroughly explores, by means of experimental selves (characters), some great themes of existence" (1986, 142). In adopting this approach to the novel, Kundera is accepting the Heideggerian view of human existence—specifically, that it doesn't make sense to talk about a self that exists apart from a historically determined situation in the world. For Kundera, as well as for Heidegger, *human being* is primarily *being-in-the-world* and not Descartes's self-sufficient "I," which is centered in itself.

In an interview, Kundera suggests that his own novels might be seen as "phenomenological" (1986, 32), i.e., as novels which attempt to show us something about our being-in-the-world as self-conscious beings. Again following Heidegger, he also says that such novels are needed because the prevailing scientific and technological thinking, which has "reduced the world to a mere object of technological and mathematical investigation" (3), obscures our everyday being-in-the-world. In Heidegger's phrase, scientific and technological thinking have led to "the forgetting of being," and for Kundera, a good novel is one which helps us to overcome this "forgetting." Such a novel shows us an unknown aspect of our existence in the world, and in doing so opens up new possibilities for our existence.

Hoping to overcome our "forgetting," in *The Unbearable Lightness of Being*, Kundera asks us to meditate on the "unbearable lightness" of human existence. The main character, Tomas, is a doctor in Prague, and he is a postmodern intellectual who thinks that the key to human existence is the unbearable lightness of a world in which everything happens but once. What is "unbearable" is the thought that whatever exists but once is without value or significance. If I only once strut and fret my hour upon the stage and then am heard no more, I signify nothing. And the same is true of everything else. Furthermore, if this is my situation in the world, I cannot know what to want; for example, if I haven't existed before, how can I know whether I should get married at this particular time? Finding myself in the midst of such a contingent world, I seem to be without weight, and thus there is something unbearable at the center of human existence.

According to this meditation, what rescues us from despair is the thought of "recurrence" or "return," and thus at the start of the novel we are presented with Nietzsche's idea of "eternal return"—the idea that "everything recurs as we once experienced it, and that the recurrence itself recurs ad infinitum" (1984, 3). That the idea of "return" is important to us seems undeniable. For example, if a race riot happens only once in Los Angeles, we tend to regard it as a fluke, of no significance; but if it happens again, the situation seems heavier, worth paying attention to. The same is true in our thinking about personal relationships: a one-nighter is regarded as an insignificant fling, not worth writing about; but if a man returns to the same woman night after night, we celebrate his behavior in "true love" poetry. We also celebrate the life of a man who has returned to the same job day after day for twenty-five years, and if that man thinks he will be "born again," he can take himself very seriously. Kundera sums up by pointing out that the thought of recurrence is tied inextricably with three others: what is recurrent is necessary, and "only necessity is heavy, and only what is heavy has value" (33).

Given such associations, human beings have tried to create a heavier world—a world governed by the eternal return. Both language and ritual approximate this heavier, more significant world. But they were only the beginning, and in the modern world, with its emphasis on rational rule following, specialized roles, and fixed, standardized procedures, existence has become much heavier. This is what we see in modern bureaucracies, but, as this example suggests, life in the heavier world is made possible only by a trade-off: for in gaining the heavier existence of eternal return, we must sacrifice adventure, novelty, and individual freedom. The same trade-off is obvious in the life of the man who gives up chasing and begins returning to the same wife night after night. With "the love of his life," he becomes heavy and significant, but he no longer experiences adventure, novelty, and freedom. In general, the heavy life of return pins the individual down, and so it is also perceived as a "burden." Thus, in fleeing from unbearable lightness, we run into the burden of heaviness. Tomas seems to suggest that what we want is a light-heaviness, but since this is impossible we are typically dissatisfied with our existence in the world.

This meditation on lightness and heaviness is illustrated in Tomas's life and also in the lives of the other main characters: Teresa, who becomes the love of Tomas's life; Franz, the schoolteacher; and Sabina, the artist and mistress of both Tomas and Franz. Each of these characters senses the unbearable lightness of human existence in the world, and each deals with it in a different way.

The key to Tomas's life is that he usually wants to "make heavy go to light" (1984, 196). Thus when we first meet him we learn that he has divorced his wife and separated himself from the rest of his family, opting instead for a life of womanizing and "erotic friendship" (12). It is an accidental meeting with Teresa, who taps into his "poetic memory" (208), which causes him to return to a heavier existence. But even then he maintains a great many light, erotic friendships, causing Teresa a great deal of suffering. Did Tomas—and do others who fall in love—simulate his love for Teresa in order to overcome the unbearable lightness of being? Postmodern Kundera isn't sure, but he does suggest that a love relationship provides the best middle ground between unbearable lightness and the burden of heaviness: lying beyond the "it must be" of the natural and human worlds, "love is our freedom" (236).

Teresa escapes lightness through her relationship with Tomas, but also through her relationship with the family dog. Since the un-self-conscious dog is still a part of nature, a life in harmony with its needs produces endless repetition and a sense of heaviness, a natural heaviness without conflict. Kundera praises dog love, and he shows that it is one of the better ways of escaping lightness, perhaps superior to love for another human being! Kundera's point is that we should give up on Descartes's goal of making mankind "the master and proprietor" (288) of nature and instead try to live in harmony with nature—although Kundera also emphasizes that a full return is impossible for a self-conscious animal.

Tomas's attitude toward lightness is contrasted with that of Franz, a modernist schoolteacher who is constantly trying to turn lightness into heaviness. Like other modernist intellectuals from Plato to the present, in experiencing the world, Franz is constantly searching for universal essences and necessary rational truths. If such essences and truths could be located, existence would become very heavy, and we could know the world and what to do in it. The problem is that while searching for universal essences and timeless truths, we overlook the contingent particulars that actually exist in the world. Specifically, while trying to shove people into our conceptual boxes, we ignore their concrete uniqueness and see them in terms of abstract categories that exist only in our heads.

Here, modernist Franz is contrasted with postmodern Tomas, who, because he accepts that everything happens but once, has no interest in locating universal essences and timeless truths. The difference is illustrated in their approaches to women: Tomas is an "epic womanizer" (201) who is interested in the particular qualities which make each of his lovers unique and who is thus open to the light reality that he actually experiences. Franz, on the other hand, is a "lyrical womanizer" (201) who searches for his lovers' resemblances to the Ideal Woman (based on his image of his mother) and who is thus closed off to the unique human being who is actually before him. Yearning for heaviness, Franz even keeps his eyes closed in bed! In setting up the contrast, Kundera clearly sides with Tomas's postmodern approach to the world, and he shows that Franz's heavier approach inevitably blinds him to light reality.

Whether he is describing Franz's thinking about his wife, mistress, or revolutionary politics, what Kundera emphasizes is that modernist intellectuals like Franz "[have] always preferred the unreal to the real" (120) and thus "understood nothing" (119).

If Franz grew up with a strong yearning for a well-known, heavy world, the artist Sabina wants only an unknown lightness. She thus lives a life of betrayal—where "betrayal" means "breaking ranks and going off into the unknown" (91)—betraying her father, her husband, the communists, and even her countrymen. And whenever a lover like Franz tries to get heavy with a proposal, she again sets off for the unknown, that is, for the unbearable lightness of being.

Because she represents an extreme way of dealing with a world in which everything happens but once, Sabina is perhaps the most interesting character in the novel. Particularly interesting are her ideas about art. To begin with, she calls for an art that forces human beings to think about the fundamental lightness of existence, and for this reason she rejects realism as well as kitsch. For her, as for a postmodern like Lyotard, realism is merely art that presents the world that collective common sense believes in, the heavy world that "everybody knows." She prefers cubism over realism because in cubism the pretense of such a heavy world is gone, and in its place are many individual points of view, many contingent, light worlds instead of one heavy world. Rather than silencing individual voices, cubism celebrates them by showing us that there is beauty in their lightness. Thus, like the novel as an art form, cubism helps to make possible "the paradise of individuals."

In developing her postmodern aesthetic theory, Sabina asserts that "beauty is a world betrayed" (110). Specifically, it is an artistic image that betrays the heavy world of Totalitarian Truth—an image that helps us to see the fundamental lightness that underlies any collective human order that we believe in. Beauty is thus an image of a peaceful landscape with a blotch of spilled red paint on it, or an idyllic still life of apples, nuts, and a tiny, candlelit Christmas tree, showing a hand ripping through the canvas. In such paintings, much like dadaist paintings just after the First World War, the heavy collective world is betrayed through the addition of something incongruous, something not in harmony with conventional representations of the world. In such art, our faith in the heavy rational order is smashed, and the fundamental lightness of existence again shines forth. What appears is an individual voice, the Other that exists beneath the official collective voice.

On the other hand, Sabina finds kitsch intolerable, and it is the main subject of Kundera's "novelistic essay" in the sixth part of the novel. In discussing kitsch, Kundera emphasizes that it is art aimed at producing a "categorical agreement with being" (248). What this means is that kitsch is an art that reassures us that the author of Genesis was right when he said that "the world was created properly, and that human existence is good, and that we are therefore entitled to multiply" (248). Kitsch reassures us by showing us a world in which the unacceptable is totally denied. As Kundera puts it, "Kitsch is the absolute denial of shit, in both the literal and the figurative senses of the word; kitsch excludes everything from its purview which is essentially unacceptable in human existence" (248). Here we might note that while Dostoevsky's Ivan Karamazov thought the main theological problem was the existence of moral evil in God's world, for Sabina the problem is aesthetic—the existence of ugly shit in God's world!

Kitsch is the art that says it isn't so, that, for example, Jesus did not shit. Here we should think of some of the kitsch images of Jesus—of the gentle Son of God, bathed in a golden aura, speaking love to innocent young children. Such images totally fence off the unacceptable shit of existence, and they do so by appealing directly to the heart. As Kundera says, "When the heart speaks, the mind finds it indecent to object. In the realm of kitsch, the dictatorship of the heart reigns supreme" (250). But in order to overwhelm the mind, the feeling induced by kitsch must be shared by the multitudes, and for this reason kitsch is based on images which are engraved on the memory of a group—e.g., of a happy family opening presents around a Christmas tree, first love, the death of the family dog. Such images not only create strong emotion, they also bring people together, and Kundera says, "The brotherhood of man on earth will be possible only on a base of kitsch" (251). But in doing so, it leaves no room for the individual voice, for the unbearable lightness of existence—and thus Sabina hates it.

In her art as well as her personal life, Sabina wants only to betray the heavy collective world. But at the end of the novel, we learn that although she has betrayed her father, her husband, all of her lovers, the communists, and her countrymen, she still cannot face the total and unbearable lightness of her individual existence in the world. Instead, we find her living with an elderly couple in America, part of the happy family sitting around the kitchen table and telling stories in the evening, just as it is pictured in the kitsch that Sabina despises. Kundera's point is that no human being can fully embrace the unbearable lightness of being.

But, for Kundera, the greater problem today is the human being who wants to embrace greater heaviness and who, as a result, is willing to persecute the individual voice. This is what Kundera emphasizes in describing the major historical event which dominates the novel—the

1968 communist invasion and later occupation of Czechoslovakia. Here what we see is a group of human beings who, in their flight from lightness, have set up a society which is controlled by a single collective voice, specifically, by the voice of the Party, Party art, totalitarian kitsch, and an endless repetition of the Party line, keeping everyone marching in step in the May Day parade, with heavy but frozen smiles. Kundera also shows us that this social situation was backed up by a secret police who attempted to stifle all deviance through an invasion of private life. In this kind of society, there is plenty of Eternal Return with the same clichés and poses repeated over and over, but there is little humor, irony, novelty, imagination, adventure, or play. It is a society which has clamped down on the beauty of the Other, and it is also the kind of society which appears in all of the novels discussed in this section. The only difference between the villagers in *The Painted Bird*, on the one hand, and the communists in *The Unbearable Lightness of Being* and the capitalists in *Being There* and *Breakfast of Champions*, on the other, is that the villagers are not armed with rational technology.

Aside from its theme, *The Unbearable Lightness of Being* is an important work because it shows us the promise of a postmodern approach to the novel. In writing this novel, Kundera, like Kosinski and Vonnegut, has abandoned the modern starting point that the novelist must first hold a mirror up to nature. And like Vonnegut, he has also abandoned the idea that the reader must be presented with an orderly story in which events are presented in a logical way, with a beginning, middle, and end. Here, too, the narrative is broken, tangled, and filled with repetition, and we learn about the main character's death before we learn about the last few years of his life. Kundera also keeps interrupting—to make some personal comments about his characters or perhaps to give us his novelistic essay on kitsch. Like Vonnegut, he wants to keep reminding us that we human beings are responding to works of the imagination, not to truth. The characters are only lightly described (we know nothing about Tomas's physical appearance and nothing about his childhood), and the descriptions are given only to help the reader understand the character's existential situation in the world, not to tell us what he is "really like."

In short, neither the story nor the characters are designed to give us the Single Rational Truth about the world; rather, they serve as a meditation on human existence—specifically, on the unbearable lightness of being and how human beings can deal with it. Here a meditation has replaced the mirror, and the goal of the meditation isn't to preach Totalitarian Truth, but to open up possibilities for our own existence in the world.

And finally, in this novel Kundera suggests that the model human being isn't the modernist who is trying to capture essences and truth; rather, he is a human being who faces the contingency of his existence, while being guided by a sense of beauty. The model is Tomas, who, when he sees a contingent but beautiful love, hangs on to it and makes it a major motif in his life. The problem of human existence isn't how to capture the world in rational categories; it's to take contingency and give it a beautiful shape.

Note

1. I took this quote from the *L.A. Times*, a number of years ago. I regret that I can no longer locate the citation for it.

4 From Modern to Postmodern Art and Architecture

[A painting is like] a transparent window through which we look out into a section of the visible world.

> — Alberti, fifteenth century
> (Minor 1994, 61)

Art should have no other guide than the torch of reason.

> — David, eighteenth century
> (Canaday 1959, 30)

Show me an angel and I'll paint one.

> — Courbet, middle nineteenth
> century (Canaday 1959, 103)

I do not want to represent nature; I want to recreate it.

> — Cézanne, late nineteenth
> century (Canaday 1959, 344)

[My art-project isn't] make-believe . . . [it's] the real life.

> — Christo, late twentieth century
> (Maysles, Zwerin, and Maysles
> 1978)

From the beginnings of Western art in ancient Greece, artists were especially preoccupied with representing reality, and this preoccupation continued throughout the modern period. The idea that a painting could somehow show us the truth about the world was greatly reinforced by the discovery of perspective at the end of the Middle Ages, for with perspective the artist could provide the illusion of a three-dimensional world on a two-dimensional surface. Thus in the Renaissance Alberti defined a painting as a "window" on the world. As in modern literature, the representations that appeared in the artist's window kept changing throughout the modern period, but not the goal of providing an accurate representation of the world. Because they saw themselves as truth-finders, all of the artists in the modern tradition, whether neoclassicist, romanticist, realist, or impressionist, did "objective studies" of their subjects before painting them, and even a romantic artist like Constable could say that

> Painting is a science and should be pursued as inquiry into the laws of nature. Why, then, may not landscape be considered as a branch of natural philosophy, of which pictures are but experiments? (Gardner 1970, 658)

In the first part of this chapter, we will look at the history of artistic representation throughout the modern period, beginning with Poussin and David; and as in the chapter on literature, in discussing this history we will also be concerned with the gradual awareness of the limits of a modernist approach to the arts. Then we will turn to Lyotard's postmodern aesthetic theory, contrasting it with Kant's modern theory, and finally to a discussion of postmodern art and architecture.

The Early Modern Tradition: Neoclassicism

In the seventeenth century Poussin was the leading French painter, and in his window we find a world which is well ordered, peaceful, and without the details of a particular time or place. Poussin also wrote an influential treatise on painting that called for a "grand manner" classicism in which artists would show only "great subjects" (e.g., battles, heroic action, and biblical scenes), while excluding extraneous detail and anything "low" (i.e., everyday life) (Gardner 1970, 594). The key to this kind of art is "restraint," "moderation," "balance," and "good taste," and this is what we find in David's first paintings a few years later. But then, while still attempting to provide an "imitation of nature in her most beautiful and perfect form" (Gardner 1970, 639), David developed a much stricter art, as is illustrated in his neoclassical paintings such as *Oath of the Horatii; The Death of Socrates; Lictors Bringing Back the Bodies of His Sons to Brutas; The Death of Marat;* and *Le Sacre.* In these paintings David was governed by the belief that "Art should have no other guide than the torch of Reason" (Canaday 1959, 30), and thus they enable us to see how the celebration of reason influenced early modern art. We can also see the same kind of world that we found in Racine's neoclassical tragedy, *Phèdre.*

To begin with, it is a world which is written in the language of mathematics. In *The Oath of the Horatii* (see Figure 1), for example, everything is based on the number *three:* specifically, there are three simple arches in the background and three triangular shapes in the foreground; three unemotional soldiers on one side and three emotional women on the

84

Fig. 1. Jacques Louis David, French (1748–1825), *The Oath of the Horatii*, 1784, Oil on canvas, 130 x 168 in, Collection of the Louvre. © PHOTO R.M.N.

other side; and a stern Roman father at the center of everything, throwing three swords out to his soldier sons. According to the story being illustrated, the father is ordering his sons to fight, risk their lives, and kill for their country, even though they will be killing one of their own in-laws (the fiancé of one of the weeping women in the painting). If you were a postmodern, you might think of the father as a power-hungry patriarch, or perhaps as the Führer ready to sacrifice some more German boys, but David pictures him as a noble human being who should be revered and followed. The father's noble message is that his boys must do their rational duty for their country, rather than yield to sissy emotion. And like all of the human beings in the painting, the father has an idealized, youthful body with a solid, geometric shape. The painting's message—that human beings should fight down selfish passion while striving to do their duty in a rational universe—is simply and clearly stated in the painting.

As we saw in *Phèdre*, what makes everything simple and clear is that there is no room in a rational window for the "lowly" everyday world that we actually experience. Specifically, there is no room for change, complicated historical developments, the clutter of confusing detail, complex human beings, lower classes, and the difficulty of clearly separating good and evil. This everyday world continues to be ignored even when David drops legendary subject matter and looks through his rational window at contemporary events and people. For example, in *Le Sacre*, Napoleon appears as a noble and handsome young genius, rather than as the uncouth and portly little man who was responsible for the deaths of thousands of human beings, and Josephine appears as a pure young thing, rather than as the poorly preserved forty-one-year-old not noted for sexual purity.

Since David worked for Napoleon, perhaps this was to be expected, and much more revealing is David's *The Death of Marat*. Here the subject was a complicated, sordid, almost ludicrous contemporary event—the stabbing death of a leader of the French Revolution in his bathtub, where he spent his days writing on an improvised table while soaking his psoriasis. The murderer was a sneaky but clever woman who managed to get by security; she had been sympathetic to the revolution but was now morally outraged by Marat's excessive use of the guillotine. She murdered him to stop it; afterward she was guillotined herself. In David's rational window, all of this is reduced to a simple, neoclassical tragedy—a few essential details, a quiet, somber mood, and a noble hero who dies a blissful stoic death while doing his duty for his country. As in *Phèdre,* everything is simple and solid and clearly outlined in the language of mathematics, and there isn't a hint of historical or moral complexity.

In presenting such a world David is not just playing around or simply trying to make a living. His purpose is serious, and he believes that "the arts must contribute forcefully to the education of the public" (Gardner 1970, 640). If, as a skeptical postmodern, you were to ask him just what his "moral education" consisted of, perhaps you would first be told that it is an education that encourages people to control their passions and do their rational duty. This idea of rational duty was also preached in *Phèdre,* and it is also illustrated in *The Oath of the Horatii, The Death of Marat, The Death of Socrates,* and *Brutas.*

If you were to ask David why the actions described in these paintings are examples of "rational behavior," he would be hard-pressed to answer you with a rational argument. Indeed, as Hume pointed out, nothing is contrary to reason, not even the preference for destroying the whole world over the scratching of your finger. The point here is that the notion of "rational duty" is hopelessly vague and does not provide any specific moral prescriptions for living in the world. On the other hand, if rational duty is emotionally associated with patriotism and "doing what's good for France," it seems to have some kind of specific meaning. And, ultimately, it is patriotism that David's art education appeals to; as he said, he wanted to create a "devotion to the fatherland" (Gardner 1970, 640). Since, in the twentieth century, it has become clear that such devotion has been connected to massive slaughters, today we doubt its value as a sound moral guide, but Napoleon did not hesitate to put David in charge of France's cultural affairs.

To conclude: In order to see what the early modernist celebration of reason led to in art, it is convenient to contrast David's rational window with Rembrandt's window, which was opened onto the world a century earlier, in a country which was not convinced that "reason saves." To begin with, where Rembrandt showed us a less orderly, more detailed everyday world of working human beings, David shows us a highly general, purified world of nobility. And where Rembrandt showed us human beings who were unique and flawed individuals with bodies subject to the whips and scorns of time, David's human beings have little individuality, and they have bodies that are eternally young and ideal. In Rembrandt's self-portraits, for example, we see the face of a unique individual, at first younger and confident, and then older, with more wrinkles and wear; and in a picture of his companion (*Danae*), we see the naked body of a paunchy, middle-aged woman, rather than a perfectly proportioned and eternally young Josephine. (And unlike

David's passive helpmates, Rembrandt's beloved is a woman who has a will of her own, as John Berger has noted [Berger et al. 1972, 58].) Individualized characteristics, sometimes even ugliness, can also be seen in Rembrandt's paintings of religious subjects. On the other hand, even in David's more relaxed portraits of his friends, we continue to see the ideal form rather than a flawed and concrete human being. The point here isn't to discuss the various causes of these differences, which would include Dutch capitalism and protestantism, but only to emphasize what cannot appear in the rationalist window of early modern art. If David is also contrasted with Goya, who lived at the same time but not in a country devoted to reason, we can see what else cannot appear in David's window: strange, imaginary forms, madness, and the brutal horrors of the everyday world. What we see in David is what we saw in Racine: reason excludes.

Romanticism, Realism, and Impressionism

Although they still believed in truth, the romantic artists didn't think it could be found in David's paintings, and they were the first to argue that the rational window excludes a deeper truth about human beings and the world they live in. As has been noted in the earlier chapters, for the romantic, this "deeper truth" can be found only if we get closer to the nature that exists beneath our rational minds and civilized forms. Here the assumption that nature has a rational order is dropped. The new assumption is that if we set aside our rational thoughts and simply intuit or directly experience nature, we will discover its truth. Given this faith—the modernist faith that it is possible to have direct contact with something other than language—the romantic artists thought that their pictures of the world were more "realistic" than those of the neoclassicists.

Although there are variations, none of the romantics show us anything resembling David's clear, solid, and orderly nature. The language of mathematics, of Newton's orderly cosmic clock, cannot be found in the romantic paintings of Géricault and Delacroix; think specifically of Géricault's *Raft of the Medusa* and Delacroix's *The Lion Hunt* (see Figure 2) and *The Death of Sardanapalus*. In such paintings, we encounter a disordered world characterized by violent motion, broken, irregular lines, and intense, overflowing and expressive color, rather than David's static platonic forms, subdued color, and geometric shapes. What we see is that nature is now in flux, and its purpose is no longer clear. And instead of David's self-controlled, rational essences, we find suffering, and

Fig. 2. Eugène Delacroix, French (1798–1863), *The Lion Hunt*, 1860/61, Oil on canvas, 76.5 x 98.5 cm, Potter Palmer Collection, 1992.404. Photograph © 1994, The Art Institute of Chicago. All rights reserved.

sometimes mad human beings who are controlled by their emotions; and they have tortured and dying bodies. Much closer to Darwin than to Rousseau, these romantic paintings minimize the difference between human beings and other animals: savage lions and savage human beings fight side by side, and often horse and rider seem to be one, twisting in violent motion. As Delacroix said:

> It is evident that nature cares very little whether man has a mind or not. The real man is the savage; he is in accord with nature as she is. (Gardner 1970, 646)

Here, and in many romantic paintings, what is suggested is the worldview of Schopenhauer and Nietzsche. As was mentioned earlier, for Nietzsche, there is no rational design behind what appears; rather, there is a blind chaos of dissatisfied and competing wills to power. And in this view, the human being is no longer a unique creature with a rational essence; in other words, the will to power is also the driving force in human life.

In the sublime art of Turner, Constable, and Frederick, the romantic window shows us a more peaceful, mystical world, but it is not a world that can be grasped through human reason. Nor do the exotic settings and great literary heroes of romantic art show us anything of the contemporary, everyday world that the artist was living in. Here you might consider Delacroix's *Liberty Leading the People,* a romantic picture of a contemporary event, the 1830 revolution in the streets of Paris. Despite the violent movement, gun smoke, death, and recognizable street types, Delacroix can show us only an allegory in which beautiful, half-naked Liberty is leading the French people to the Promised Land. In comparison to *The Death of Marat,* in *Liberty* we see a world in motion. It is a world which is dominated by passion, but since the romantic still thinks he must present universal and timeless truth, he remains far removed from the particular, historical, and everyday world.

Like Stendhal and Balzac, the realists who followed the romantics did look closely at the world around them. As Courbet said:

> To be able to translate the customs, ideas and appearances of my time as I see them—in a word—to create a living art—this has been my aim. . . . The art of painting can consist only in the representation of objects visible and tangible to the painter. . . . Show me an angel and I'll paint one. (Canaday 1959, 103)

Here the artist is no longer concerned with universal and eternal truth; rather, he wants us to see the historically determined truth of his own time. And instead of angels and idealized heroes, he shows us the everyday street people in the world around him. For example, in *The Stonebreakers, Burial at Ornans,* and *Two Girls on the Banks of the Seine,* we no longer see rational or emotional essences but individualized and flawed human beings submerged in the contemporary world. They are neither dressed up, nor being led by Liberty.

The realist tradition reaches a striking conclusion with Manet's *The Olympia* (see Figure 3). Here, instead of the traditional sweet and beautiful reclining nude, we see one of the coarser Parisian whores staring right back at us, without a submissive smile, perhaps waiting for an offer, totally indifferent to David's eternal moral values. And in order to give us the truth about her, Manet tries to be scrupulously objective; like Flaubert in describing Madame Bovary, the artist here strives for an impersonal presentation of his subject, describing her as a scientist might describe an insect. Thus, where David wanted to show us an eternal rational essence while telling us an uplifting moral story, Manet is content to show us an everyday, flawed human being who lived at a particular time in history. And instead of moralizing, Manet is content to

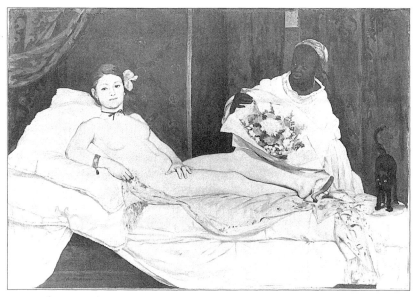

Fig. 3. Édouard Manet, French (1832–1883), *The Olympia*, 1863, Oil on canvas, 51.25 x 71.75 in, Collection of the Musée d'Orsay. © PHOTO R.M.N.

tell us: "This is the way it is." It can also be noted that where Delacroix wanted us to see eternal emotional truths, Manet wants to keep all emotion out of the picture. Seduced by the ideal of scientific objectivity, Manet thinks that by suppressing emotion and moral judgment, he will be able to give us a more accurate picture of the world.

But Manet, like the other artists who became impressionists, later realized that presenting the truth is more difficult than the window-on-the-world tradition had assumed: for a distinction can be drawn between *what* an artist sees and *how* he sees it. In other words, the impressionists concluded that artists could no longer ignore the subjective element in the window, and so they attempted to show us the truth about how the world appears to a perceiver. In pursuing this truth the impressionists emphasized that objects appear differently at different times of the day under different conditions of lighting, and thus their paintings specifically focus on momentary appearances of the world—not a general view of the object, but a specific view of the object at 9:05 a.m. Eventually, Monet shows us not one but several paintings of haystacks, revealing how he saw them at different times of the day. What should be emphasized here is that the impressionists were still working within the window-on-the-world tradition, and they continued to think of themselves as scientists, but now the artist is a scientific expert on optical sensations, and he identifies truth with how an object appears to the eye of a perceiver at a particular moment.

But why assume that a painting focusing on a momentary optical sensation gives us the truth about how the world appears to us at a given moment in time? This assumption makes the eye omnipotent, and it ignores the role of the mind—specifically, of thought, emotion, and a particular language—in shaping how the world appears to us. Based on this view of perception, Monet's water lilies are nothing more than merging patches of color, without solidity or hard outlines. But is this the way water lilies really appear to us? Or has Monet demonstrated that since our pictures of the world are shaped by linguistic descriptions, this odd picture of water lilies is shaped by a rather odd way of describing perception? Postmoderns favor the latter explanation.

The Decline of Modernism and
the Origins of Postmodernism

By the end of the nineteenth century, the entire modernist, truth-showing, window-on-the-world tradition was obviously in question. In taking impressionist theory to its extreme, in giving us pictures of how water lilies, haystacks, and cathedrals appear to the eye at a brief moment, Monet shows us formless flashes of color rather than the solid and distinct water lilies, haystacks, and cathedrals that we actually experience in the world. Cézanne in particular began questioning the impressionist reduction of the world to a momentary optical sensation—to a *transient view* of the world which ignores the world that we *think* exists—and in his late-nineteenth- and early-twentieth-century paintings he attempts to restore shape and solidity to the world that is seen through the window. Thus, in his *Mont Ste-Victoire* paintings, we see more than passing color patches; we also see the hard outlines of solid houses and a solid mountain behind them. In his attempt "to make of impressionism something solid and durable" (Canaday 1959, 339), Cézanne still thought of himself as a scientist who was trying to capture the object's essence, but he is no longer a scientist who is certain of what he sees. As is sometimes pointed out, instead of giving us a painting which boldly asserts, "This is what I see," Cézanne gives us a painting which doubtfully asks, "Is this what I see?" (Barbara Rose, quoted in Hughes 1991, 18). Also, Cézanne's paintings of an object are based on several different views of it, involving memory and conscious thought, not just the eye. Again, what is now clear are the limits of basing a view of the world solely on what appears to the eye, and thus painters like Cézanne begin considering how the world appears in thought. As Kant argued against the empiricists, how human beings perceive the world is influenced by the active, organizing power of the mind—passive, optical impressions are only a small part of the story.

But what is most radical in Cézanne is that he gives up the project of providing an accurate representation of nature. He is still concerned with presenting the truth, but he now feels that in order to convey it, he must distort what comes to him through the window. At this point he abandons the ancient tradition. Although he was still a truth-revealer, his art and his famous sentence—"I don't want to represent nature; I want to create it"—point clearly toward a postmodern conception of art.

Cézanne's new way of thinking about art is much more radically developed by Picasso and the cubists, and Picasso says directly: "I paint forms as I think them, not as I see them" (Hughes 1991, 32). What is particularly new in Picasso's art is that instead of showing us how an object appears from a single perspective, he shows us how it appears from many different perspectives. In abandoning single-point perspective, Picasso followed Cézanne and attempted to reveal an object's essence by showing how it appears from many different angles. As was mentioned in discussing Virginia Woolf, the hope here is that many different views of an object will add up to an objective view of it. But Picasso's still lifes, musicians, and women do not reveal truth. Rather, they reveal what Nietzsche, William James, and Virginia Woolf were revealing at about the same time: that all views of the world are subjective fragments based on time, place, and change, and that no matter how many views we are aware of, there is still no reason to suppose that they add up to an objective view of things.

What these cubist paintings suggest is the limits of all attempts to represent the world accurately. In many later cubist paintings, the situation is even worse—we can't even find a recognizable object. When cubism first got under way, there were at least several fragmented views of a recognizable object, but in some of the later paintings, there are simply aspects of "a something I know not what." Such paintings remind us of what postmoderns emphasize: the great gap between the descriptions in the thinker's head and the objective reality outside. We will return to Picasso's cubism in discussing postmodern aesthetic theory, but here it should be emphasized that cubism points toward a new way of thinking about art. In developing this new way of thinking, Juan Gris, one of the most famous cubists, says: "My aim is to create new objects which cannot be compared to any object in actuality" (Gardner 1970, 691). And a few years later, Magritte shows us a painting of a pipe, while reminding us, "This is not a pipe."

Although the attempt to represent nature came to an end and it was becoming clear that how we describe the world controls how we perceive it, the modernist hope that the artist could present truth lived on, but now the truth was seen as psychological. To some extent this hope began with the romantics who attempted to express emotional truth. But the romantics were concerned with universal emotions, whereas the late modernist hopeful were attempting to probe their individual psyches. The hope was that the artist could have direct contact with his own soul—i.e., perhaps art can be a window onto the individual soul. Vincent van Gogh's art is an attempt to provide such a window, and in paintings such as *Starry Night*, he is not trying to give us a picture of nature or of how nature appears to the eye; rather, he wants to show us how a unique human being feels about nature. In other words, the artist now wants to show us his deepest self. As van Gogh said: "Instead of trying to reproduce exactly what I have before my eyes, I use color more arbitrarily so as to express myself more forcefully" (Gardner 1970, 678).

In the twentieth century this modernist hope of expressing subjective truth continued with surrealism, with artists attempting to show us a human being's deepest unconscious fantasies, desires, and complexes. In the 1940s, the same tradition led to abstract expressionism, so that Jackson Pollock, under the influence of Jungian therapy, thought he had expressed his self in his splashes of paint in *Lavender Mist Number 1, 1950*. And yet, as was emphasized in earlier chapters, there is no reason to think that a human being has direct contact with his soul, and no reason to believe that any kind of self-description, whether linguistic or pictorial, reflects that soul. Specifically, it is difficult to see why anyone would think that *Lavender Mist Number 1, 1950* is somehow a window on what Pollock was "really like" underneath the language he thought in. And if we conclude that art doesn't give us a window on either the subjective or objective world, the modernist truth-telling tradition in art is over.

In reviewing this modernist tradition in art, we should here briefly focus on the changing representations of the individual self. As in literature, there is a basic shift from universal, solid, and self-sufficient individuals (i.e., the rational and emotional essences which we find in neoclassical and romantic art) to particular, malleable, and socially shaped individuals (i.e., human beings without essences who are the products of contingent historical forces—whom we find in realist art). At the end of the nineteenth century, in van Gogh and Munch we encounter confused individuals who seem to be little more than bundles of tortured emotion. Nor is there anything solid in impressionism and cubism; and

in surrealism the individual becomes a mysterious, irrational unconscious. Eventually, in one of Magritte's paintings, we see a bowler hat
sitting on top of nothing! And at the end of the tradition, we see
Giacometti's *City Square* sculpture, which shows us isolated human beings about the size of toothpicks, just small pieces of mass in blind motion. Later, Giacometti carried his people sculptures to exhibitions in his
pocket! And it is certainly difficult to find anything resembling a centered individual self in the paintings of abstract expressionism.

To conclude, with a growing awareness of the shaping power of language, the illusion of truth, the limitations of reason, and the impossibility of locating a centered individual self, a postmodern approach to
art began to develop. It especially got under way when early-twentieth-
century dadaists began sneering at the entire modern tradition, and especially at the idea that more reason will save us. Believing that a rational civilization led to the First World War, the dadaists thought we should
turn against a rational approach to art. Better to be childlike and put a
mustache on the *Mona Lisa,* said Duchamp, who also thought that we
should forget about Roman fountains and instead turn to the aesthetics
of the urinal. Even more important to later thinking about art, Duchamp
turned against the idea that an artwork is marked off from other objects
by something unique to "art"; instead of such essentialism, he shows us
that it is only the context of history and language that causes us to single
out some objects in our environment as "art."

A few years later, in the 1930s, Magritte shows us that although we
think we are responding to objective reality, we are responding only to
language and symbols. Like Wittgenstein at the same time, he wanted
to overcome our confusion, and to be helpful he reminds us that his
picture of a pipe is "not a pipe." In *The Treason of Images,* he also helps us
by placing the word "door" against the picture of a horse, thus reminding us that there is only an arbitrary relationship between words and
the things and images they stand for. Finally, coming at the end of a long
tradition, Magritte gives us *The Human Condition.* Here we see a painting of a painting on an easel standing against a window. But this window opens not onto the world but onto the rest of the picture, thus reminding us that the whole idea of a picture window was a mistake. To
paraphrase Derrida, there is nothing outside the picture.

Postmodern versus Modern Aesthetics

Before discussing distinctively postmodern art and architecture, we
should look at aesthetic theory, beginning briefly with Kant's modernist
aesthetics and then more fully discussing Lyotard's postmodern aes-

thetics. In presenting his theory, Lyotard is especially preoccupied with the twentieth-century avant-garde art of Picasso, Braque, Duchamp, de Chirico, Malevich, and Newman, and what he emphasizes is that it is an art that no longer provides what Kant would call the experience of "beauty." But before discussing Lyotard we need to return to Kant's *Critique of Judgement.*

First, it should be noted that, during the eighteenth century, a modern approach to aesthetic theory was developed, and this approach centered not directly on the objective properties of an artwork or natural object, but rather on how we *experience* it. Writing toward the end of the century, Kant's starting point is still this focus on aesthetic experience, and he follows the earlier thinkers in distinguishing between two kinds of aesthetic experience, the experience of beauty and the experience of the sublime. He also follows the earlier thinkers in claiming that, in both experiences, there is a pleasure "independent of all interest" (1986, 42), i.e., a pleasure which, unlike the pleasures of sex or moneymaking, is not tied to the satisfaction of the spectator's private desires and interests. Finally, for Kant, as for his predecessors, both pleasures can be produced by natural objects and artworks. But Kant also insists that "the concept of the sublime in nature is far less important and rich in consequences than that of its beauty" (1986, 93), and he scarcely mentions the sublime in art.

The experience of beauty is what counts, and in discussing it, Kant begins by noting that it is a response to an artwork or natural object which at first seems to be without purpose or meaning. Unlike a newspaper article, a beautiful rose or *Hamlet* is difficult to quickly reduce to a clear-cut meaning or purpose, and yet, with contemplation, it does begin to seem purposeful, i.e., to be in harmony with a rational nature that wants unity, order, and purpose. Kant calls this aesthetic situation "purposiveness . . . without purpose" (1987a, 84), and he argues that it is the object's lack of an immediate meaning or purpose which invites aesthetic contemplation. What happens when we contemplate an object such as a rose is that its form seems so perfect that we feel it must have been designed to please a rational nature that tries to understand the world— which would be the case if it were designed by another Rational Nature. When we experience an object in this way, its form produces a pleasurable inner harmony, as imagination and reason come together in "free play" (1986, 58). As was mentioned earlier, in this theory the emotions and senses are not the key to why we find an object beautiful; what counts is the object's formal perfection, which, in satisfying our desire for unity, order, and purpose, makes reason feel "at home in nature" (64).

For Kant, sublime aesthetic experience—think of looking up and see-ing a vast Saharan desert—differs from the experience of beauty because the sublime experience is not based on a form that eventually makes sense to reason. Rather, in focusing on the sublime desert, I am up against a formlessness that does not seem preadapted to my rational attempts to figure out the world. Thus there is pain in a sublime aesthetic experi-ence—the pain of being confronted with something that does not make sense to human reason.

Yet Kant claims that such a sublime experience also involves a disin-terested rational pleasure. This is because a sense of "infinity" enters my mind when I contemplate the vastness of the desert, and when it does, I am reassured that reason is supreme. Kant's point here is that since the desert, like everything that comes to us from nature, is finite, the idea of infinity must come from within a rational mind. Thus, in contemplating the desert, I have a sense that reason rules nature, and it is this thought which gives me pleasure, according to Kant's extremely intellectual aesthetics. Notice, however, that sublime aesthetic experi-ence does not reassure me that I can understand nature, only that as a rational animal, I can rise above its apparent confusions.

The reason Kant thinks beautiful art is important and scarcely men-tions sublime art is that he believes that human beings need to be reas-sured that reason delivers truth. In the *Critique of Pure Reason* Kant ad-mitted that we can never actually know if nature is rational, so we have to admit that the use of reason *might* be futile. Yet in the *Critique of Prac-tical Reason* Kant argues that we can live a moral life only if we follow reason. Thus in the *Critique of Judgement* he says that the experience of beauty is important because, by making "reason feel at home in nature," it reassures us that we are right in trying to organize the world in terms of reason. Sublime art offers no such reassurance and is therefore not important.

In *The Postmodern Condition* and *The Inhuman,* Jean-François Lyotard develops a postmodern approach to aesthetics which accepts Kant's start-ing point, but which reaches different conclusions. To begin with, Lyotard follows Kant in distinguishing sharply between beauty and the sublime, and he also agrees that in the experience of beauty, there is "an accord between the capacity to conceive and the capacity to present an object that corresponds to the concept" (1992, 10). Finally, as Kant said, in sug-gesting that there is an agreement between the world and the concep-tual order in our heads, beautiful art reassures us that there is nothing wrong with our attempts to understand and order the world in terms of our rational concepts and theories. But while Kant thought this reassurance was positive and thus praised beautiful art, Lyotard thinks it is negative, and thus he praises sublime art.

Before explaining why, we should note that Lyotard's discussion of the sublime differs from Kant's in two ways: first, Lyotard ignores the connection between the sublime and what is overwhelmingly vast (the desert) or powerful (a hurricane); and second, he focuses on sublime art rather than sublime nature. On the other hand, he agrees with Kant that in the experience of the sublime, we are confronted with an object that fails to correspond to our preconceived view of the world. In Lyotard's words, sublime art presents "the existence of something unpresentable" (1992, 11)—it presents us with something that we cannot already conceive of. In making this claim, Lyotard has his eye on avant-garde art precisely because it is, above all, an art which confronts us with the limits of our ability to reduce the world to our rational concepts.

To see why Lyotard thinks this is important, it is convenient to again focus on Picasso's cubism, which comes at the beginning of the avant-garde tradition; here we will focus specifically on a recent exhibition of a number of Picasso's paintings of the women in his life. The exhibition was called "Picasso's Weeping Women," and most of the paintings provide good examples of Picasso's cubism. In analyzing cubism, we have already mentioned that by presenting us with several fragmented and subjective views of his subjects rather than a single, rational view, Picasso forces us to think about the limits of what we can know about the world.

To see what this means with regard to the weeping women paintings, imagine how they might appear to a sexist. To begin with, he is not reassured that his views of women are accurate. But more than that, these strange images of women suggest that although he may share his view with friends and even with an entire society, it is no more objective than many other possible views (see Figure 4). As his eyes move around the women in these paintings, trying to capture them conceptually, looking to see if a particular wife fits one of his preconceived stereotypes of women—bitch? whore? Madonna? mother?—he is constantly frustrated. Could his present ways of classifying women *not* be objective? This same and disturbing thought could also occur to his wife Angel, and it could even be followed by another: that since her present self-concept is merely another subjective fragment, merely another viewpoint like those in the paintings, she might even think of another, more fulfilling self-concept and start rebelling against being Angel. The point here is that Picasso's nonrepresentational, multiple-perspective paintings force human beings to think about the great gap between what they can conceive of and what might be real. And by undermining the faith that our already-

Fig. 4. Pablo Picasso, Spanish (1881–1973), *Weeping Woman*, 1937, Oil on canvas, 59.7 x 48.9 cm, Tate Gallery, London, Great Britain. © ARS, NY.

formed concepts are objective copies of what is real, these paintings open up the possibility of moving beyond a stereotyped way of life.

The aesthetic consequence of such art is both sublime insecurity and pleasure. First, there is the insecurity of realizing that we have nothing certain to hang on to, and this involves the painful thought that we don't know each other or even our selves. But at the same time there is a sublime feeling of pleasure, not simply from the realization that reason can exceed the confusion that comes to it from the world, but also from the experience of escaping from a dull and clichéd conceptual prison—the pleasure of experiencing freshness and novelty. Here we should note that whatever confirms collective common sense may be reassuring, but it is also boring, "the same old thing." In Picasso's nonrepresentational, sublime art there is the pleasurable excitement of dealing with the unknown. It is the pleasure of playing with, rather than capturing, Kosinski's "painted bird."

But Lyotard not only praises the liberating potential of sublime art; he also thinks it should be valued more highly than the representational, beautiful art that reassures us of our rational thinking about the world. As to the question, why?—in other words, why should we be discouraged from placing a high value on our concepts and theories?—Lyotard's answer is close to what Heidegger and Kundera would say, and it is an answer that can be traced back to Nietzsche.

Specifically, Nietzsche argued that Kant and modern scientists were wrong in distinguishing between concepts and metaphors, wrong in claiming that concepts differ from metaphors in that they are objective and provide a rational basis for our theories about the world. For Nietzsche, the distinction is bogus because both concepts and metaphors are formed by focusing only on some similarities shared by objects, while ignoring their differences. Just as "all men are dogs" focuses only on sexual similarities while ignoring differences, so the concept of "dog" is formed by focusing only on some similarities while ignoring differences. In other words, for Nietzsche, all concepts are subjective fragments rather than objective truth, and this includes the concepts of modern science.

The point that Lyotard stresses is that in forming our concepts and theories, we are inevitably excluding something that doesn't fit. Again, reason excludes. And for Lyotard this not only means that scientific theories cannot be objective, they can also have negative social consequences. In explaining why, we can again go back to Nietzsche, specifically, to his claim that our creation of concepts and theories springs not from a spiritual love of truth but from an animal will to power. In other words, reason, which excludes, is inevitably tied to a desire to dominate, and in trying to classify and make things and people similar, we are simply trying to make them be the way we want them to be. Furthermore, when we act on our concepts and theories, we are trying to force the world into our desired order; typically, we do so in a group, and, as in *The Painted Bird*, "we" is formed at the expense of "them." Things or people which don't fit into our conceptual or theoretical order must somehow be coerced, "normalized," or perhaps eliminated. For Lyotard, as for Foucault (who will be discussed in the next chapter), it doesn't matter which theory we hold—whether that of an Eastern European peasant, a Nazi, a Marxist, a capitalist, or a modern psychologist—whenever we act on the theory, it will be at the expense of the Other. Specifically, the theory of Eastern European peasants led to the persecution of a small boy; theoretical Nazism led to the death camps; and theoretical communism led to Stalin's purges. And at present, theoretical capitalism, with the aid of modern technology, is aimed at the elimination of the traditional cultures around the world, while theoretical psychology is after all forms of social deviance.

In this extreme view all attempts to actualize our concepts and theories have the same result: they force sameness into the world while persecuting diversity, and thus they produce "terror" (1992, 16). As Lyotard says, all attempts to reduce the world to a rational order "totalize" in this way, and thus Kant's Enlightenment dream of a universal man leads to the elimination of individual men, as it did in David's and Racine's neoclassical art. In short, reason inevitably serves the will to power, and it cannot tolerate the Other.

Thus we need Picasso's sublime weeping women paintings because, by reminding us of the limits of our totalizing ways, they help us to overcome the terror of the twentieth century. We need his art because, unlike beautiful, representational art which reassures us that we've got it all figured out and that our conceptual order is wonderful, sublime nonrepresentational art reminds us of the pleasure of dealing with what cannot be boxed up, the pleasure of dealing with the Other. It reminds us of what we embraced as children, the pleasure of imaginative play without closure. This kind of pleasure is also felt when we bring our own "Other" into existence—as when we overthrow our traditional self-concepts and project something new into the world.

To summarize the shift from a modern to a postmodern aesthetics: for Kant, it was obvious that reason's new scientific and moral concepts were giving human beings truth and greater freedom, while also eliminating the superstitious beliefs that prevented human beings from coming together. It was also obvious that a strictly rational approach to life had nothing to do with an animal will to power which was bent on swallowing up anything that was different. Thus Kant called for a representative art that gives us the experience of beauty. But for Lyotard, writing at the end of a bloody twentieth century in which rational, bureaucratic, and scientific societies have often been obsessed with eliminating the Other, what is needed is a nonrealistic art that gives us the experience of the sublime. Today, it is easy for many of us to share Lyotard's worry about what Weber has called "the iron cage" of reason;

it is also easy to agree with Lyotard's "equation between wealth, efficiency, and truth" (1984, 45)—to agree with

> No money, no proof—and that means no verification of statements and no truth. The games of scientific language become the games of the rich, in which whoever is wealthiest has the best chance of being right. . . . (45)

On the other hand, the sublime isn't everything, and it is difficult to believe that our social problems can be solved without an art that gives us beauty, and thus unites and reassures us that we are right in trying to develop a more democratic society. Beautiful images are important because they bring us together and encourage us to harmonize our diverse interests, which is essential in a democratic society. As we saw in the last chapter, Kundera shares Lyotard's distrust of an art that unites and assures us of a rational world, but Kundera added that we probably even need kitsch (which Lyotard particularly despises) because it brings together diverse human beings and makes social life possible. Here you might think of the idealized images of Abraham Lincoln, "the American who freed the slaves." In short, Lyotard is right in pointing to the great value of a sublime art, but his "war on [all] totality" (1992, 16) seems absurd, and his urge to separate art from beauty is as coldly rational as Kant's desire to separate beauty from sex.

Postmodern Architecture and Art

Before discussing distinctively postmodern art, we should look briefly at postmodern architecture and, first, at the modern tradition which it seeks to replace. As was classically illustrated in Versailles, the modern tradition in architecture is based on a strong faith in reason, and early-twentieth-century architects were especially preoccupied with the utopian idea that reasonable buildings would somehow lead to reasonable and humane human beings. Toward this end, Adolf Loos wanted to get back to the pure, rational shape, eliminating anything superfluous or ornamental; in Loos's words, "The evolution of culture is synonymous with the removal of ornament from utilitarian objects" (Hughes 1991, 168). Loos's love of a sober, plain white wall with nothing but windows is clearly illustrated in the back of his Steiner House, which was built in Vienna in 1911. But the concept of a strictly "reasonable building" reaches its high point with the International Style and the attempt to produce structures so simple and functional that they could be used for any purpose, by anyone at any time, anywhere. We can see this style in countless corporate buildings across the United States—buildings which are recognizable by their steel frames and glass curtain walls. Because the modern architect's goal was to create a square box of rationality in an otherwise irrational city, these buildings often seem foreign to the environment in which they are situated, but this was not a problem because soon the whole world would be filled with such rational structures. As Le Corbusier, the high priest of the International Style, put it, "The right angle is lawful, it is part of our determinism, it is obligatory" (Hughes 1991, 187). In this view, even houses are "machines for living."

In order to hurry up this more rational, utopian world of the future, Le Corbusier was anxious to wipe out a large section of an "unhealthy and antiquated" Paris (188), which was just too full of irregularity, clutter, and compromise. His own plan, as illustrated in his *Drawing for the Voisin Plan* (see Figure 5), shows us a much cleaner Paris with perfectly straight lines and right angles.

Another modernist, Ludwig Mies van der Rohe, could find no reason to be concerned with the individual human being while building a rationalist utopia. As he said, "the individual is losing significance; his destiny is no longer what interests us" (Hughes 1991, 181). Nor was the human body of significance in a rational, modern utopia. And since the building and its furnishings must be considered as "one thing" (199), as Frank Lloyd Wright had said, furniture was reduced to a rational essence that no body could be comfortable in. Chairs that would torture any human body show us the comic side of the extreme modern desire for a more rational world. In sum, in trying to create a universal rational man, modern architects were, like Racine, David, and modernism in general, willing to ignore individual humans, their history, and even their bodies. Again, reason excludes.

It is also of limited utility, and perhaps the failure of the modern dream—that rational structures would eventually cause human beings to live rational, humane, and happy lives—was most clearly revealed on a single day in St. Louis with the officially planned destruction of the Pruitt-Igo housing project, where rational buildings existed side by side with irrational behavior, hallway knifings, rampant muggings, and rapes.

The postmodern approach to architecture developed out of the failure of the modern dream. It developed out of the realization that a world reduced to rationality, simplicity, and functionality—or, in Kant's words, unity, order, and purpose—is not enough to produce humane and happy human beings. To see where it differs from modern architecture, we can begin with the Gehry House in Santa Monica, contrasting it to Wright's Robie House in Chicago. In the Robie House, everything—e.g., the design of the living-room ceiling, which continues into the dining-room

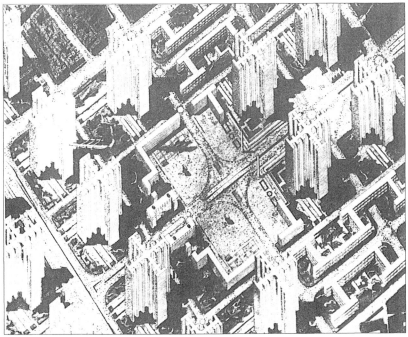

Fig. 5. Le Corbusier, *Drawing for the Voisin Plan*, 1925, Akademie der Kunste, Berlin. © 1996 Artists Rights Society (ARS), New York/SPADEM, Paris.

ceiling; the low horizontal lines that correspond to the lines of the prairie; the design of the stained glass windows that unites all of the windows of the house—shows an overwhelming desire for unity. Once inside, we quickly find the center, the hearth, and we also note that all things are at right angles. It is a house in which reason prevails.

The Gehry House (see Figure 6), on the other hand, shows absolutely no preference for a simple geometrical order and rational unity. To begin with, it is a traditional 1920s bungalow which Gehry has surrounded with a radical 1970s exterior, in such a way that the exterior and the bungalow can both be seen at the same time. Not only that, but the exterior is made of diverse industrial materials such as corrugated aluminum, chain-link fencing, and unfinished plywood, and it has cubistic windows arranged in such a way that one looks through the new addons to see the old house!

Once inside, there doesn't appear to be a center, and many of the lines are not at right angles, thus leaving the viewer searching in vain for anything resembling vanishing points. If the viewer stands in the kitchen and looks toward the street, he is facing the corrugated exterior

Fig. 6. *Frank Gehry House,* Santa Monica, California, Tim Street-Porter, photographer. © Tim Street-Porter/ESTO Photographic, NY. All rights reserved.

wall; in the opposite direction, he sees an exterior bay window of the old house; and if he looks up, he sees the sky, while all the while standing on what used to be the driveway. Furthermore, since one house is within another house and glass is used as a ceiling, what is "internal" and what is "external" become questionable. The kitchen is on the exterior of the old house and the interior of the new house! This house is obviously not one which makes reason feel at home in the world, and it has nothing in common with Wright's belief that there must always be an organic unity. Rather, it is a celebration of diversity and muddling through.

Many of the postmodern characteristics found in the Gehry House are also found in Portman's Bonaventure Hotel in Los Angeles. Here, too, there is nothing which would make a rationalist feel at home in the world, beginning with the entrance. Once you have found it (there are three, two of them on the sixth floor) and are in what you think is inside, you are not greeted with a simple rational order in which everything falls into place. Just finding the registration desk is no easy task, and it takes a maze of color-coded lines on the floor (the colored lines were added several months after the hotel's opening) to help modern old-timers find their way. If you look around for a clear sense of direction, you instead see streamers hanging from the ceiling, protruding balconies, an artificial lake, gardens with all kinds of plants, round elevator shafts, and endless shops and restaurants—a whole, cluttered postmodern city. If you move through the maze to your room, you'll be required to take an elevator, which will shoot you through the ceiling onto the exterior of the hotel. But once the door opens, you'll be safely back inside. As this brief description suggests, it is a hotel which reminds reason that it is not enough for dealing with a postmodern world.

At the same time, the Bonaventure reminds us that while an unadorned building with straight lines and right angles may satisfy the rational ego, there is also an aesthetic pleasure which comes from playing around in a world that lacks rational clarity. Even Kant saw this when, against the neoclassicists, he argued that the imagination is more important to art than rule following; but since modern architects such as Loos, Mies van der Rohe, and Le Corbusier were still burdened by the command to follow reason, they had no time for playing around in the world. But in a postmodern world the burden is gone, and thus it becomes possible to escape from the deadly seriousness of the modern ego that wants to save the world through more rationality. It becomes possible to imagine a more open world in which we play with the Other, instead of obsessing on a unity in which the Other is sacrificed to reason.

In the visual arts, the development of a distinctively postmodern view of our situation in the world began to take shape in the 1960s, and it is first expressed in the pop-art paintings and sculptures of Hamilton, Rauschenberg, Warhol, Lichtenstein, and Oldenberg. What makes pop postmodern is its lack of concern for contact with anything that exists beyond our human-made world. It doesn't attempt to give us the truth about God, nature, or the self. Rather, it simply focuses our attention on the mass-produced world of consumer products and media images, without attempting to give that world a rational shape. In major pop works such as Hamilton's *Just What Is It That Makes Today's Homes So Different, So Appealing,* Rauschenberg's *Retroactive II,* and Lichtenstein's *Drowning Girl,* we see a human world that has been created not by nature but by the mass media—by television, ads, and the comics. In this world, there are no "natural" emotions. Rather, there are mass-produced media emotions, whether the impersonal apathy that comes from the endless repetition of images and constant channel changing, which is what Hamilton and Warhol show us, or the emotion of "true [media] love," which is what Lichtenstein shows us.

With regard to true media love, in Vonnegut's *Breakfast of Champions,* we see it illustrated in the life of the devoted and self-sacrificing secretary of an insane, unloving Pontiac dealer, a woman "willing to agree about anything with [her man], no matter how difficult or disgusting, to think up nice things to do for him that he didn't even notice, to die for him, if necessary, and so on" (1973, 160). In *Drowning Girl*, Lichtenstein gets to the source of such love in *Young Romance* comics; specifically, he shows us a blow-up of a scene in which another devoted and self-sacrificing heroine is drowning while saying, "I don't care! I'd rather sink— than call Brad for help!"

Andy Warhol is undoubtedly the most famous postmodern artist, and in showing us endless cans of Campbell's Soup (see Figure 7), big Brillo boxes, or the same image of Marilyn Monroe again and again and again, Warhol is simply showing us the human-made, mass-produced world that we live in, without trying to make us see any deep truth about it. Moderns, of course, see him as trying to tell us something, but they can't seem to agree on what it might be: Is he criticizing a consumer society which offers nothing but more of the same junk, as Gardner says? Or is he perhaps praising democratic capitalism, where everybody gets the same bottle of Coca-Cola for the same price, as Danto says? Warhol himself describes his art as all "surface"; "There's nothing behind it" (Workman 1990). When he was later asked what he was trying to "express," he also said, "nothing."

Through his emphasis on graphic techniques, two-dimensionality, repetition of the same images, and advertising techniques, Warhol is reminding us of the postmodern point that human beings cannot get beyond their symbols. He also shows us that, ultimately, it is our symbols and language that determine what is and what is not "art." As Duchamp insisted earlier, it is the context that surrounds the object— the museum, art history, and the descriptions of both—that determines whether it is art, not the object itself. What makes Warhol's argument against an essentialist view of art so striking is that he shows us that even the most commonplace objects, objects seen every day on a supermarket shelf, can, with the right kind of language, be turned into "art."

Warhol also suggests that the artist has nothing to say about a deep individual self. As he said, he has no concern with expressing his self, and, in place of Marilyn Monroe's unique essence, he shows us a lot of media images—just the same made-up face, with no suggestion that it reveals a deep identity beneath the surface. Here the public, mass-produced surface is all there is.

The topic of personal identity is also taken up in the photographs of Cindy Sherman and Barbara Kruger. Sherman calls her images "self-portraits," but when we look at them, we cannot find anything resembling a private, centered self. Instead, we are exposed to many "Cindy Shermans," and all of them are obviously cultural constructs, derived

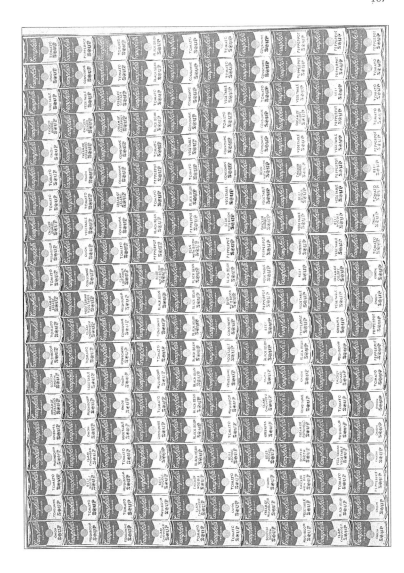

Fig. 7. Andy Warhol, *200 Campbell's Soup Cans*, 1962, Oil on canvas, 72 x 100 in, Private Collection, Courtesy Leo Castelli Gallery, New York. © 1996 Andy Warhol Foundation for the Visual Arts/ARS, New York.

from attempts to center her existence on media images. What we see is a series of poses—copies of copies (with slight variations), with no original in sight. It is the world of Baudrillard's simulacra—a symbolic world of copies, without a trace of an original referent.

The pictures and words of Barbara Kruger also take a postmodern view of personal identity. She is particularly concerned with sexual identity and what gives shape to it, and she mocks Descartes's "I think, therefore I am" explanation with "I shop, therefore I am." In other words, it isn't a woman's private thoughts that give shape to the identity which she comes to believe in. Nor is it an essential female nature. In one of her photographs, we see only a woman's hat with nothing but three fingers holding it and "I am your reservoir of poses" (1990, 35) under it.

Like other postmodern feminists, Kruger sees sexual identity as constructed by a traditional public language, and in her photographs, she reminds us of a sexist language which tells girls that they should play with dolls, be passive before male power, and make themselves pretty. As she says in one of her photographs, this kind of language has produced only a "mistaken identity," and she sometimes suggests that art critic John Berger is right when he claims that the key to the mistake is a language that says *"men act and women appear.* Men look at women. Women watch themselves being looked at" (Berger et al. 1972, 47). Thus, in one of Kruger's photographs of a classically sculptured female head, she has the female say: "Your gaze hits the side of my face" (1990, 62). In another photograph, she tells women directly that they will not find an acceptable identity by looking in any mirror, whether in the bathroom or in the male eye. And in a third photograph, a female face in a shattered mirror reminds women: "You are not yourself" (1990, 31) (see Figure 8). With regard to male identity, in one picture we see a young girl with pigtails, feeling the flexed muscle of a little boy who is playing tough, and Kruger tells them both: "We don't need another hero" (1990, 86).

Finally, in trying to overcome the traditional descriptions and images which have shaped women, Kruger wants women to know that beneath the issues of abortion, birth control, and human rights, there is simply a fight over who is going to control the woman's body. In urging support for these causes, she succinctly says: "Your body is a battleground" (1990, 58).

Christo is one of the most interesting postmodern artists, and we'll conclude with a discussion of his "art-projects." These projects—including surrounding several Caribbean islands with six million square feet of floating pink fabric; hanging a huge orange curtain between two moun-

Fig. 8. Barbara Kruger, *Untitled (You Are Not Yourself)*, 1982, Photograph, 72 x 48 in. Courtesy: Mary Boone Gallery, New York.

tains in Colorado; constructing an eighteen-foot-high, twenty-four-mile-long white nylon fence in Northern California; and stringing thousands of giant umbrellas across mountains and rice fields in Southern California and Japan (see Figure 9)—are also major social projects. They are important because they ask us to think in new ways about art and what we should do in the world.

Christo's film *Running Fence* (Maysles, Zwerin, and Maysles 1978) documents his Northern California project, and it shows us a particularly interesting postmodern form of "art." Briefly, the film begins with

Fig. 9. Christo, *The Umbrellas*, Japan-USA, 1991, California Site. Photograph by Neil Anstead.

Christo's initial attempts to get permission from the Northern Californians to construct his fence over their property, and it shows us the necessary legal hearings, with Christo and his wife Jeanne-Claude dealing with bureaucrats and landowners. After permission is granted, we see the actual construction of the fence—a project which requires a great many workers, complex technology, and heavy construction. Then we see a few shots of the long, curling white fence against the Pacific Ocean, and the film concludes with an epilogue that tells us that it was taken down two weeks after completion, with all the materials going to the ranchers whose land it crossed.

So what are we supposed to think about this kind of art? To begin with, Christo wants us to drop our traditional idea that art must provide us with the truth about the world. As he says in the film, his art-project is not "make-believe" . . . [it's] "the real life" (Maysles, Zwerin, and Maysles 1978). In other words, the *window*—whether on the external world or on the soul—is gone. Nor does a Christo art-project have anything to do with forcing a rational order upon the world. In taking us beyond such modern thoughts, Christo also asks us to stop thinking of art as a finished product of some kind, and especially not as a product that "endures throughout the ages." Rather than a finished product, we should think of art as a process—as a beautiful living project rather than a dead thing.

There are forms in Christo's art—a big white fence, a huge orange curtain, and hundreds of giant yellow umbrellas—but these forms are only a focal point and not what ultimately counts. Unlike the permanent forms we find on museum walls, Christo's forms are temporary, and their beauty is intimately tied to a natural setting. These forms also have a short life, not only because the rational ego's desire for permanent forms (asphalt, bureaucracy) is at the root of our ecological and social problems, but also because what counts most is not a permanent form, but rather the project of making the world beautiful.

Given this artistic goal, Christo knows that he cannot work alone, and many of his projects engage the interest and help of a large number of people: the greater the number, the better the art. It doesn't matter if some locals are negatively involved and make fun of "a ridiculous art-fence," as long as they and the rest of the community are thinking about the importance of beautifying the world. Actually, if the art-project creates fights, so much the better—especially when the mass media get involved—for then the whole community's attention is focused on making the world beautiful, for a change.

Obviously, the success of such a project requires a special kind of artist. First, he must have imagination and be able to create a new, sublime image. But a Christo world-beautification project requires a lot more than a creative imagination; it also requires practical know-how—the giant fence, curtain, and umbrellas have to be constructed with the aid of engineers, technology, and an enormous workforce. Finally, it requires exceptional social skills, as is illustrated when Christo and Jeanne-Claude negotiate with the dozens of bureaucrats, politicians, specialists, and property owners. In short, a Christo art-project requires much more than an alienated artistic dreamer; it also requires social and practical intelligence of the kind which enabled Christo to raise $26 million for his umbrella project after being in the country only a few years. As Yankees like to say, for a better world we need know-how as much as an artist's dreams.

What is impressive about Christo's postmodern art is that it manages to bring together a large group of human beings, without the presence of the Other. They come together while thinking about how to beautify the world around them, and they play while doing so; in the Southern California and Japan umbrella project, thousands played in work teams while spending a few weeks erecting hundreds of giant umbrellas. For those who saw it in Southern California, and were thus part of the art-project, what they saw were desert hillsides and valleys transformed into a magic yellow playground. Of course, there is no serious truth telling in this kind of art; nor is there any attempt to squeeze the world into a permanent rational order. Instead of the strict, rational organization desired by modern architects, Christo calls for a more relaxed, imaginative organization of the world. And while such organization does require reason and science, both are subservient to the artist's imagination.

The reason we conclude this section on postmodern art with Christo is that he shows us some of the positive possibilities in a postmodern artistic viewpoint. When people first encounter postmodernism, the negative seems to dominate—e.g., no truth, no self, the terrible problem of the Other, the ugly will to power, and reason leading only to terror. But once again, truth is a burden, and throwing it aside opens up the possibility for a less rigid, more playful, aesthetic organization of human life. Without the burden, all things are permitted—even an artwork which consists of a desert-dry countryside filled with thousands of human beings playing around with some giant yellow umbrellas.

5 Human Nature, Evolution, and a History of the Modern World

Twentieth-century social theory has had a major impact on the shift from a modern to a postmodern way of thinking about our situation in the world. Specifically, several major social, historical, and anthropological studies have supported postmodern ideas about human nature, language, reason, and the historical development of the modern world. In this chapter we will focus primarily on the studies of three leading twentieth-century social theorists: the German sociologist Max Weber; the American anthropologist Clifford Geertz; and the French historian (or "genealogist") Michel Foucault. Although Weber wrote first, for our purposes it is convenient to begin with the anthropology of Clifford Geertz.

Geertz and Symbolic Anthropology

Geertz is a "symbolic anthropologist" who takes a "semiotic" approach to culture (1973, 5). He thinks of a "symbol" as a sign that is human-made, arbitrary, conventional, and shared, and he thinks of "culture" as a system of symbols that gives shape to a human life. Geertz's ideas about culture and human beings are most fully developed in *The Interpretation of Cultures,* and in what follows we will focus mainly on that book. In particular, we will focus on his ideas about human evolution, the species nature of *Homo sapiens,* and why individual *Homo sapiens* think, feel, and act as they do.

With regard to our species nature, Geertz is especially concerned with challenging the Enlightenment concept of a universal man. This is the concept of a creature who has a full and substantial human nature, a fixed nature that, by itself and unmodified by culture, gives determinate shape to how he thinks, feels, and lives in the world. Geertz argues that nineteenth- and twentieth-century anthropologists have searched all over the world for universal man but haven't found him. Specifically, the search for "cultural universals"—i.e., beliefs shared by all human societies—has turned up nothing substantial. Instead of universal man and species homogeneity, the search has revealed a wide diversity of specific human types who don't universally agree on anything: not on what is real, what is good, what is right, or what is beautiful. As Geertz points out, when believers in cultural universals are faced with this lack of evidence, they are forced to rise to a high level of abstraction in order to defend their position. For example, instead of focusing on the particular beliefs that humans have, they tell us that all human societies have "religion." If they were to focus on the actual beliefs of Aztecs, Christians, and Buddhists, the "universal" would vanish. What remain are particular religious beliefs which are not shared by all societies. The same is true of beliefs about "marriage," "property," and "shelter."

This lack of cultural universals strongly supports the postmodern claim that our nature does not give a determinate shape to what particular *Homo sapiens* come to think, feel, and do in the world. In discussing this point Geertz emphasizes the contrast between the "complete" nature of lower animals and the "incomplete" nature of *Homo sapiens*. Specifically, where lower animals inherit many specific behavioral tendencies, *Homo sapiens* inherit only "extremely general response capacities" (1973, 46). Other than a few reflex actions, our nature does not give us any specific behavioral instructions. In other words, whereas lower animals are naturally programmed to live only one kind of life, malleable human beings "begin with the natural equipment to live a thousand kinds of life" (45), e.g., as Eskimos, Aztecs, Tutsis, or middle-class Americans.

In focusing on this contrast between lower animals and *Homo sapiens*, think of the fixed and stereotypical way that wild dogs go about getting their dinner, as contrasted to the countless ways that human beings go about it. And think of the fixed and stereotypical way that dogs go about reproducing themselves, automatically following the same genetically controlled pattern, as contrasted to the countless mating rituals found in the human world. In humans only the lust for genital stimulation is innate, while the stimulus that sets it off, e.g., the kind of personality and body type, and even what part of the body (feet in classical, aristocratic China), varies greatly around the human world. So does the way the sexual impulse is acted out, through what kind of ritual, pattern of behavior, position, etc.

This same contrast between fixed and flexible behavior is illustrated in the aggressive lives of lower animals and human beings. Think of your response to a threatening stimulus as contrasted to my dog's. When my dog is threatened by another male, he immediately engages in fighting or fleeing behavior, and in both cases the behavior pattern is relatively fixed and stereotypical. If he fights the pattern begins with low growls, a display of canine teeth, circling, and then attack, when he specifically goes for the nape of the other dog's neck.

Now think of how you might respond to a threatening stimulus, say, if one of your students were to pull a gun on you. Subjectively, you'd probably experience varying degrees of fear and rage, but this wouldn't be followed by any fixed, automatic pattern of behavior. You *might* respond in several different ways—e.g., you might offer him a higher grade; turn for help to a student who does have a higher grade; yell; talk quietly to him about his future; rush him; throw something at him; plead for mercy; or take out your own gun and shoot him first. The important point is that you are not naturally programmed to respond in a specific way, and how you do eventually respond has nothing to do with specific bodily instructions and nearly everything to do with symbolic cultural instructions.

In short, even when it comes to natural functions like getting our dinner, reproducing ourselves, and dealing with a threatening stimulus, we cannot rely on our essential nature to give us specific instructions. Rather, our behavior needs to be guided by the particular symbolic descriptions that we have internalized. In supporting this strong, anti-essentialist position, Geertz goes so far as to say that, given our lack of specific behavioral tendencies, we are "the animal most desperately dependent upon such extra-genetic, outside-the-skin control mechanisms, such as cultural programs, for ordering [our] behavior" (1973, 44). Unlike other animals, we live in an immense "information gap" (50), a gap between what our body tells us to do and what we need to do in order to survive. And if this gap isn't filled by symbols, and especially by linguistic descriptions of the world, we will be "unworkable monstrosities" (49).

Of course, other animals need to learn how to respond to natural signs in their environment in order to survive, but, given their relatively complete bodies, they need to learn far less than human beings. Above all, they do not need to learn a complex system of arbitrary and conventional signs. Since human beings lack innate controls over behavior, we "desperately" need to internalize such a system in order to manage our lives. Thus Geertz thinks of "culture" not only as a system of symbols but as a "set of control mechanisms—plans, recipes, rules, instructions (what computer engineers call 'programs')—for the governing of behavior" (44).

In responding to Geertz's anti-essentialist view of our "incomplete" or "unfinished" (46) nature, students typically raise the following question:

If human beings don't have any natural ways of behaving in the world, how could our early ancestors have survived? After all, at first they did not have language, and yet they did manage to feed, defend, and reproduce themselves, or else we wouldn't be here. So how can Geertz say that we lack natural ways of behaving in the world?

Geertz's intriguing answer to this question is an account of the evolution of *Homo sapiens* (a species which came into existence from one to three hundred thousand years ago) from *Australopithecus* (a genus which came into existence four to five million years ago). The major differences between the two: *Australopithecus* was only about four feet tall, was bent over in posture, had a less flexible hand, and above all had a brain only about a third the size of *Homo sapiens'* brain. Despite these differences—and this is crucial for Geertz's argument—*Australopithecus* possessed the rudiments of culture, e.g., stone tools for hunting (some of which have been dated back 1.7 million years). Since primates don't hunt by nature, the tools and accompanying hunting strategies must have been cultural adaptations that were passed down from generation to generation, extra-genetically. So were the other major cultural developments which gradually accumulated, such as fire, clothing, the incest taboo, family organization patterns, religion, art, and so on.

In discussing this evolutionary history, Geertz emphasizes that the development of *Homo sapiens* was not an all-or-nothing event, where one day there was only relatively simple *Australopithecus* and the next there was complex *Homo sapiens*. Rather, there was a long period of more than a million years during which cultural traditions were in existence and the body type of *Homo sapiens* was simultaneously taking shape— and what is important is that during this long period a human-made cultural tradition started to replace nature as the selector and shaper of the evolving *Homo sapiens* body.

Notice the difference: whereas for other animals the evolving body type was selected and shaped by the natural world, for *Homo sapiens,* a world created by cultural traditions came between the natural world and the evolving body type, and this "cultural world" began to do much of the selecting and shaping. In other words, in each generation of the emerging *Homo sapiens* the evolving body type that could take advantage of the prevailing cultural world survived better than the older body type that could not. Specifically, if successive mutations produced a baby with a bigger, more sophisticated brain, that baby would be better able to take advantage of the culturally evolving system of symbols than its brothers and sisters, and it would therefore survive longer and have more offspring who would tend to inherit the bigger brain. The same thing would happen if a baby was born with a more flexible hand that could take advantage of the hunting and toolmaking cultural tradition. And notice that if this same baby were born without strong instincts, it no longer mattered to its survival. As long as it could take advantage of a cultural tradition which worked better than a natural approach to survival, the baby's body type would become the body type of the future.

The main result of this strange evolutionary history—in which, by turning to language and culture for guidance, the human being "created himself" (1973, 48)—was the emergence of an incomplete animal without instincts, but with a very sophisticated brain. Unlike the brains of lower animals, the *Homo sapiens* brain doesn't send out specific instructions on what to do in the world—but it has the capacity to easily learn and use complex systems of symbols which do send out specific instructions, and it is this symbolic capacity which has so far guaranteed species survival. On the other hand, the *Homo sapiens* brain lacks self-sufficiency, and without the support of an extrinsic symbol system it would not be able to think in an organized, conceptual way about the world. Here Geertz follows Wittgenstein in arguing that "thinking consists . . . of a traffic in . . . symbols" (45). Furthermore, since the symbols used in thinking are public and social—given to the individual by the society in which she is born—thinking is essentially a public and social activity. Geertz's final point is that the particular way an individual *Homo sapiens* brain comes to think about the world is controlled by the particular community language which is internalized. And as we have seen, here Geertz emphasizes the great diversity of ways that human beings think about the world.

Since this point about diversity is so important to postmodern anti-essentialism, we should glance at a few examples, taken mainly from Geertz's *Local Knowledge*. First, although Americans, Navajos, and Pokots (a Kenyan tribe) all receive the same sensory data when they look at a hermaphrodite, they have quite different thoughts about what they see. Americans are horrified at the very idea of an animal that cannot be classified as male or female, so they quickly perform an operation, while the Navajos rejoice at the thought of a positive supernatural blessing which will surely bring good luck, and the Pokots merely think that nature has made a "mistake" that shouldn't be taken too seriously.

We have already mentioned the diverse ways of thinking about sexual activity, and here we might mention a few more. Take the early Christian ascetics who believed that any sexual activity prevented a spiritual life, while the early Taoists believed that prolonged sexual activity was the key to a spiritual existence. Here we might also think about the positive view of homosexuality that developed in fifth-century Greece in contrast to the negative view in Persia.

Finally, even basic ideas about the human person seem to vary greatly: while Americans, for example, are horrified by the thought of being just another role-player, just another clone without individuality, in Java a major nightmare is that one might *not* play his part perfectly, thereby allowing his naked individuality to be seen. As Geertz suggests, while Americans strive to stand out as individuals above the merely conventional social play, Javanese strive to get rid of their uniqueness so that they may integrate themselves into an eternal and deeply significant cosmic play. Human beings around the world might look at the same person, but how they think about that person varies greatly according to the community language in which they think. Kant's moral advice, to treat each human being in the same way regardless of rank, is certainly not universal moral advice.

For Geertz, not only is our organized conceptual life controlled by a particular community language, so is our organized emotional life. Unlike Hume's universal man, whose life was dominated by innate emotions, the life of Geertz's incomplete man is not. As Geertz sums up, "Our ideas, our values, our acts, even our emotions, are, like our nervous system itself, cultural products—products manufactured, indeed, out of tendencies, capacities, and dispositions with which we were born, but manufactured nonetheless" (1973, 50).

Emotions are "manufactured" especially through public, symbolic models observed in church, art, films, and stories. It is through exposure to such models that an individual's emotional life takes on an organized shape, and, again, since the models vary across cultures, so do the emotions that individuals experience. We may all see the same event, but we don't all feel the same way about it. Americans might experience grief at the sight of a dead dog, while products of other cultures might only think of a good dinner. Needless to say, they won't have watched Lassie films and been told those stories about "man's best friend."

With regard to basic emotional reactions, in *Thinking through Cultures*, Richard Shweder, another postmodern symbolic anthropologist, argues that in early life human beings do experience innate, positive feelings when physically touched by other human beings. However, Shweder goes on to say that the emotions produced by being touched in later life depend on the particular community language that has been internalized, and this includes being touched by one's mother. Among the Oriya Brahmans, where children learn early to experience dread at the thought of "pollution," they also learn that they must not be touched by their mothers at certain times of the month (menstruation) because their mothers are then polluted. At such a time a mother's touch would produce horror rather than pleasure; it would feel as bad as being touched by an "untouchable" (1991, 241–65).

American students—who are largely products of romanticism, psychobabble, and television talk shows which tell them that their emotions are the most important and private thing about them—find it difficult to believe that their emotions are not "natural." This is especially the case with the emotion they take most seriously—love. But here, too, we seem to have a manufactured emotion, and what we experience in intimate relationships is not what all humans experience. Specifically, what was experienced by Homeric Greeks, who regarded love as temporary insanity, or by misogynist fifth-century Greeks, who believed "true love" was between an older man and a younger boy, is not what is experienced by American students who have been steeped in *Romeo and Juliet* and idealized love stories about a one-and-only dream partner of the opposite sex. The word "love" may have existed in these other societies, but it didn't evoke the same meaning and emotion that it evokes in present-day Americans. Here, again, an essentialist believer in universal man might ignore these specific examples and retreat to the abstract and then talk about a "pure" or "essential" love. But such abstract "love" is not what particular human beings experience. What they experience, like the person who stimulates it and how it is acted out, is a specific, symbolically shaped form of love—which is what we would expect if we accepted postmodern anti-essentialism.

Weber and the Development of Capitalism

Geertz acknowledges sociologist Max Weber as one of the major influences on symbolic anthropology. As Geertz says, Weber believed that

> man is an animal suspended in webs of significance he himself has spun, [and] I take culture to be those webs, and the analysis of it to be therefore not experimental science but an interpretive one in search of meaning. (Geertz 1973, 5)

One of Weber's major concerns was how world religions influenced the historical development of civilizations—in postmodern terms, how religious descriptions of the world influenced the lives and history of human beings. In *The Protestant Ethic and the Spirit of Capitalism,* Weber is particularly concerned with how Protestant religious descriptions influenced the origins and history of the first capitalist societies in Northern Europe and North America. His treatment of this history is important to postmodernism not only because it emphasizes the great influence of symbolic descriptions of the world, but also because it provides a powerful challenge to Karl Marx's modern economic interpretation of history.

For Weber, economic history in general divides into two major periods. During the first, very long period, moneymaking played only a minor role in social activity, and there was slow economic growth. It was slow because men didn't take everyday work seriously, preferring to play around and indulge in pleasure, and also because, in general, need (and not greed) motivated their productive behavior. Weber acknowledges that there were always a few men who engaged in get-rich-quick schemes, but he points out that these schemes—conquering the Aztecs, for example—were not enough to produce well-developed, market-based societies.

For such societies to appear—and here we come to the second stage of Weber's economic history—there must be a group of human beings who take their everyday work seriously, are no longer motivated solely by need, and engage in a disciplined, rational pursuit of wealth. In other words, for capitalism to develop there must be prudent, calculating men who think of their work as a "duty" and who also forego the more normal expenditures of time and money on worldly pleasures, thus making time and money available for reinvestment and business expansion. For Weber, greed eventually becomes a part of the story, and it replaces need as the driving force of economic behavior, but it wasn't the driving force at the start.

Weber emphasizes that early Christianity strongly condemned greed and discouraged men from taking their work seriously, and as a result it blocked the transition to the acquisitive second stage of highly productive economic activity. Jesus' "It's harder for a rich man to enter heaven than for a camel to pass through the eye of a needle," Paul's "the love of money is the root of all evil," and the general medieval view that moneymaking is "depraved" discouraged early Christians from pouring a lot of time and energy into business activity. If you were a devoted Roman Catholic in the Middle Ages, you would be told to leave the corrupt everyday world behind and instead give your time and energy to a truly spiritual life in a monastery. Moneylending, so important to capitalist development, was defined as a sin, and the last rites of the Church could be denied to a usurer. Given such descriptions of moneymaking, it is not surprising that capitalist development was slow in the Catholic Middle Ages. The reasoning was simple: if moneymaking is sinful and a moneymaker cannot go to heaven, I should not devote my life to moneymaking. Here postmoderns will emphasize that the key to this conclusion is the original description on which it is based.

But beginning with the Protestant theology of Luther a new way of thinking becomes possible, and it begins with a metaphor. When Luther was translating the Bible into German he translated the Greek word for "toil" as "calling," and in doing so was using the common Christian word in a new way. When Paul used it in Ephesians 4:1—"lead a life worthy of the calling to which you have been called"—he meant that Christians are called to live in a spiritual way; in other words, he was referring to a spiritual style of life, rather than to everyday work. But with Luther the meaning changes, as God "calls" Christians to work in the everyday world. What is important here is the idea that "work in the calling was a, or rather, *the*, task set by God" (1958, 85). The result was a new way of thinking about work: whereas, in the past, work was associated with a "curse" (as in the Garden of Eden story) or with an activity that only a slave would perform (as in Classical Greece), from the sixteenth century on, work was associated with a God-appointed task— with the ultimate meaning of one's life.

Following Luther, the language of John Calvin was even more important to the new way of thinking which made capitalism possible. He, too, told his followers that they were put on earth to glorify God through hard work at their secular calling. But in Calvinism, the duty of one's calling is associated with two other ideas: first, with the duty to live an ascetic life, and second, with the doctrine of predestination. According to the latter idea, an all-powerful God has already decided who are the saved and who are the damned. Furthermore, there is nothing the individual can do about his spiritual destiny through his own efforts or through the help of another. The believer was also told that although he could not know who specifically is damned, "most" are.

Weber argues that as a result of this way of describing the world, Calvinists took their businesses far more seriously than earlier businessmen. Since there was no way of knowing just who was damned, the typical Calvinist lived in a constant state of anxiety: "Am I one of the elect? . . . And how can I be sure of this state of grace?" (1958, 110). For Weber, the only way to escape from this anxiety, the only way to gain some kind of psychological (but not logical) assurance that one was indeed saved, was through spiritual action in the everyday world. Specifically, this required intense self-control, diligence at one's calling, and the careful avoidance of normal, spontaneous pleasures. In other words, the new religious symbols led to the kind of behavior that was needed for a capitalist and industrial revolution.

In his concluding chapter, Weber shows that as capitalist development was taking place, the prevailing descriptions that governed behavior gradually began to change from "the Protestant ethic" (briefly, all work and no play in order to glorify God and, indirectly, to gain assurance of salvation) to "the spirit of capitalism" (all work and no play in order to make more and more money). What happened in the eighteenth and nineteenth centuries was that the religious roots of the business spirit began to fade into the background while greed and the duty of moneymaking moved into the foreground. This is illustrated in the writings of Benjamin Franklin and Horatio Alger: both talk as though we *must* work hard and avoid everyday pleasure, but the ultimate goal was now simply to make more and more money. Such crass materialism is far from the spirit of the Gospels, but, as Weber says, what Protestant redescriptions eventually created was "an amazingly good . . . conscience in the acquisition of money" (1958, 176). Besides, since greed as an end in itself guaranteed further capitalist development, the lack of religion didn't matter, and eventually "time" became "money."

To fully understand the postmodern importance of Weber's theory of historical development, we need to see it in contrast to Marx's theory. As Marx says in his preface to *German Ideology,* at the root of major historical developments are new economic and social conditions. Specifically, first there are changes in a society's economic base—changes such as the discovery of coal, a new tool, or new productive relations. Then these basic changes lead to class conflicts and changes in the social relations across the entire society. Finally, as a result, changes take place in how the members of a society think about the world.

Thus in the *Communist Manifesto* Marx argues that modern capitalism began with the new economic and social conditions which came into existence at the end of the Middle Ages, especially with the breakdown of the old feudal order and the explorations of the world in the fifteenth and sixteenth centuries, which greatly stimulated trade. These changing conditions gave rise to new class relations and new institutions and eventually to a new way of thinking about moneymaking—a way of thinking which preceded and came into existence independent of language and the way a particular social group described the world. As opposed to Weber, what is crucial for Marx is that redescriptions of the world are secondary, reflecting more basic economic changes that have already taken place.

Perhaps because there seems to be something rock-solid about Marx's theory of historical development, something founded directly and obviously on basic species survival, many of the major postmoderns were originally influenced by it, including Rorty, Foucault, Lyotard, and Baudrillard. Notice the seductive logic: human beings first must get their dinner, and only after do they have time to think; and since thought seems to follow behavior, how human beings act in getting their dinner will determine how they think. One major problem with this view is establishing just how getting your dinner, by itself, determines all of your thoughts about human relationships and everything else. The problem is the claim that the cause-and-effect relationships must go from the economic base to descriptions and thoughts about the world. Another major problem is that, perhaps because he wrote under the shadow of the Enlightenment's concept of a universal man, Marx could not see the desperate and primary need for a system of symbols that organize and give meaning to our lives.

In developing this contrast between Marx and Weber, we need to turn to Marx's analysis of oppression—his attempt to trace the master-slave relationship back to economic scarcity and class struggle. His key idea is that human beings oppress one another because there is an economic payoff; under market-based capitalism this means that bourgeois bosses keep down the proletariat through low pay because they must do so in order to compete, make a profit, and stay in business. As in Marx's analysis of historical development, economic conditions are seen as all-determining, and the role of language in human life is ignored.

The reason it should not be ignored is that language, by itself, leads us to think about human beings and the world in an oppressive way. This is because language leads the incomplete animal to see the world in terms of good and bad, superior and inferior, winner and loser. In other words, language itself sets up hierarchical social divisions in our mind, and in doing so it creates a symbolic desire for social position. How many language-users can resist this desire to be "at the top"? And since the easiest way to rise is by joining a group that is putting down the Other, language-users are inclined to oppress one another rather than live as equals. Kenneth Burke, another language-oriented thinker, understood this point. He thought it was related to the negative—that is, in linguistic thought we think not only about what something *is* but also about what it *is not*. Thus the person I am thinking about doesn't just exist as someone who is "good"; she is also someone who is "not bad." Because of the negative, which comes into existence with language, the worldview of a language-user is predicated on a ranking system.

In dealing with this problem Burke tied language to an incomplete animal's need for social organization. For such an animal to have any kind of social order, symbolic moral rules are needed; but since individuals have sinful private thoughts and do things that violate these rules, they suffer from feelings of guilt and inferiority. Given such feelings, there springs a need for "redemption," and this leads to "victimage (the scapegoat)" (Burke 1968, 450). In other words, the symbolic moral rules lead to painful thoughts of evil and inferiority which are then commonly projected onto an innocent Other, as we mentioned in discussing *The Painted Bird*. We also mentioned the unifying function of the Other, and here is how Burke puts it:

> Is it not a terrifying fact that you can never get people together except when they have a goal in common? That's the terrifying thing that I begin to see as the damnation of the human race. That's how they have to operate; they get congregation by segregation. (181)

The main point here is that the symbolic need for the Other is a major part of the story of human oppression, and thus that story is not merely rooted in economic scarcity and class interests. To understand this point, we need to follow Geertz, Burke, and Weber and look at other roots which are just as "primary." Specifically, we need to look at our fundamental incompleteness and desperate need for a language to organize us, and which does so while putting an "us-them," "superior-inferior" way of thinking into our heads. Direct economic scarcity can intensify the desire to put down and oppress, but Marx was wrong in assuming that it is the whole story. What he did not understand, and what Weber, Burke, and the postmoderns do understand, is that symbolic scarcity is also "real" in human life.

To return to *The Protestant Ethic*, what this book argues is that the historical development of capitalism is largely a consequence of a new system of symbols which was created at the beginning of the modern era. In arguing that the world's first capitalists were responding to religious redescriptions of work, play, salvation, and God, and not merely to the objective economic conditions of market production, Weber brings us back to Geertz's view that human beings are incomplete animals who must live by symbols and meaning and not by bread alone.

This point seems especially obvious in technologically abundant societies like ours—societies where the majority have more than enough food, shelter, and clothing, and yet continue to ghettoize and put down the Other. This isn't to deny that economic systems set certain limits on the way human beings live in the world, but it is to deny that these "limits" are as rigid and all-determining as Marx thought. Nor does a postmodern follower of Weber have to advocate an idealist theory of history (a theory which makes mental processes primary in explaining historical change) over a materialist theory (which makes physical conditions primary). Who knows why Luther used "calling" in a new way—whether as a free mental act, or because of a kink in his brain, or a strange upbringing, or whatever. The cause could be mental or physical, and Weber's only crucial postmodern point is that it was a new system of symbols that led to major changes in a society's organized social and psychological life. Finally, in preferring Weber over Marx, the point isn't to praise a capitalist America filled with selfish greed and injustice, but only to assert that Marx overemphasized economic scarcity and underemphasized symbolic scarcity.

Foucault and the Development
of a Disciplinary Society

There is another major theme in Weber's sociology which is important in postmodernism—his theme of "the rationalization of the world." A postmodern might say that as capitalism developed in the seventeenth, eighteenth, and nineteenth centuries, the language of Calvinistic Prot-estantism merged with that of rationalism, and eventually Protestant-ism lost its hold while rationalism played an increasing role in shaping social life in Western societies. As we have seen, rationalism is the doc-trine that human life should be based on inquiry and beliefs that follow with certainty from premises and general principles, rather than from tradition, religion, passion, or the imagination. As market production began to expand in capitalist societies, rationalism also came to mean a social life controlled by increasing specialization and bureaucratization. This required human beings who would submit to restricted work lives, impersonal rules, and formalized general procedures. It also required human beings who would turn against spontaneous pleasures, personal fantasies, and individual choice and creativity. Since this more rational way of living in the world made capitalism immensely successful, We-ber felt that it would probably continue, but he was also troubled by it because he thought it meant "the disenchantment of the world." This disenchantment arises from the rational removal of God, mystery, and magic, and it also arises from a rational work life limited to narrow and specifically defined job roles which allow no room for individual cre-ativity, spontaneity, and imaginative play. It is what is found in the life of the bored bureaucrat who hates his work but goes on with it in order to purchase more material goods and raise his standard of living.

The early Calvinists, whose ideas helped to create our present situa-tion (with perhaps the most boring jobs in history), could have tolerated it because they believed in a secular, ascetic calling and also in big re-wards in the "next world." But today a great many feel differently about their ascetic work lives. They'd rather be elsewhere, but, as Weber says, they are trapped in an "iron cage." In taking this position—that the strictly rational third stage of capitalism would be governed by disen-chantment and a joyless iron cage—Weber was close to Freud when Freud wrote *Civilization and Its Discontents* a few years after Weber's death. In Freud's language, the development of rational, civilized forms requires greater and greater "repression" of all spontaneous, impulsive tendencies and fantasies, and as a consequence it inevitably produces a lot of "discontents."

In the rest of this chapter we will discuss postmodern discontent, and we can first mention the major twentieth-century historical developments to which postmoderns are responding. To begin with, developments in science have resulted in consequences which the early rationalists couldn't have imagined. Above all, science has made slaughter possible on a scale that was unimaginable in traditional warfare. The ten million deaths in the First World War would not have been possible without major scientific and technological "advances." Nor would the slaughter which took place in later wars, including Hiroshima and Auschwitz. Perhaps our first tendency is to blame these disasters on ignorance and politics rather than on science and technology, but it's hard to ignore the fact that scientific reason has armed ignorance and politics with nuclear weapons. As Vonnegut said:

> Scientific truth was going to make us so happy and comfortable. . . . What actually happened when I was twenty-one was that we dropped scientific truth on Hiroshima. (1989, 161)

More recently, we have been forced to look at another major consequence of rational scientific and technological thinking—widespread pollution and ecological destruction. Increasingly, it has seemed that the advances of the most rational species have been at the expense of less rational species, and now we are told that there is a limit to how many we can destroy without destroying ourselves. Again, we first look to ignorance and, perhaps, greed as the cause, but neither was as dangerous before the developments of modern science. We still go to the doctor, but today it is easy to associate science with death and destruction.

A third historical development has also helped to undermine our faith that "reason saves," and it is the use of science and technology by post–World War II capitalists. In particular, now that consumer capitalism is armed with science and technology, the power of capital over the world has increased to the point that, today, it seems irresistible. Before advances in television and communications technology, there seemed to be some room for escape from capitalist greed and manipulation of consciousness, but today escape seems impossible. How many of your students are not devoted to a life of consumption? How many can resist the latest media-created fads? Did any of them not become superpatriots overnight during the Gulf War? In *Postmodernism, or, the Cultural Logic of*

Late Capitalism, Fredric Jameson tells us that capital is now "colonizing" the unconscious in addition to precapitalist societies (1991, 48–49). We have already noted how this situation has influenced postmodern denials of a core self that exists independent of language and especially of television language. We have also seen that it has influenced the postmodern denial that some kind of truth might be located amidst the media-created simulacra in which we live. Here the point is that science and technology seem also to have greatly magnified the power of greed.

Another major historical development which has fostered postmodern discontent is the twentieth-century history of communism. At the beginning of the century, communism, perhaps the last great project of Enlightenment reason, seemed to many intellectuals the most sane approach to social life—a welcome alternative to an irrational capitalist system driven by greed and selfish individualism. Even in the 1920s and 1930s, many still had hope of a better, more rational communist tomorrow, and thus many of the postmoderns began their intellectual lives as Marxists. Today the old hope is gone. Instead, we have to face the fact that there has been constant oppression and cruelty within the communist world. First, there was the news of Stalin's murders and purges, then the crackdown in Eastern Europe, and today it's hard to ignore communist China's attitude toward individual human rights. With the collapse of communism in Eastern Europe and the Soviet Union, we have also seen that centralized planning couldn't even deliver the goods. But as was noted in discussing Lyotard, for postmodernism the more important issue is that communists, acting on the basis of a very rational theory, have had a terrible twentieth-century record of oppression, murder, and terror.

Given such historical developments, it is easy to see why postmoderns tend to regard reason as a problem rather than as a panacea. Under Rousseau's "return to noble savagery," reason also became a problem for nineteenth-century romantics, but for the postmoderns, the problem is far more serious. For some, the devotion to a rational social life is inevitably tied to the oppression of the Other, whether under capitalism or communism.

Writing under the influence of Nietzsche and Heidegger, Foucault is perhaps the most important postmodern advocate of this view, and beginning with his first major work, *Madness and Civilization,* he focuses directly on the negative side of the history of reason. Specifically, he wants us to see how easy it is for human beings to "confine their neighbors" in "an act of sovereign reason" (1965, *ix*). His main point in *Madness* is that as Reason became God in the seventeenth century, the voice of Unreason was silenced. Specifically, Foucault shows that as seventeenth-century Westerners became more committed to a rational social life, they greatly increased their confinement of people who had "mental disorders." Only shortly before, during the Renaissance, the voice of madness had a certain degree of freedom in European societies. Although madness was associated with evil, it was also associated with "folly" and frivolousness, with making people playful, and even with a strange sort of wisdom. As we are told in Shakespeare's plays, there is "reason in madness." Given such associations, mad people were allowed freedom to wander around the countryside, and although they were sometimes exiled on a "ship of fools," they were not systematically locked up.

But Foucault argues that this traditional, relaxed attitude changed in a rationalist seventeenth century, during which folly was forgotten and the new associations of madness became sharply negative. After the founding of the Hôpital Général in 1656, mental deviants in Paris were locked up in a prison-like institution, and at this point reason clamped down, suddenly silencing the voice of madness. Foucault also shows that since this was the time of an emerging market society, madness became associated with idleness, and thus in silencing deviance, reason was on the side of market rationality (1965, 54–61). *Madness and Civilization* won't be our major concern here, but it provides a key to Foucault's general position: that while reason serves the interests of a particular kind of social order, it does so by putting the Other into a cage.

One of Foucault's most important books is *Discipline and Punish,* and in it he traces the history of what he calls "punitive reason." Foucault focuses on how Western societies have dealt with criminals since the seventeenth and eighteenth centuries, but he is more generally concerned with the historical development of our present-day "disciplinary society," and, as in *Madness and Civilization,* with how this society treats deviance and the problem of the Other.

With regard to the history of the punishment of criminals, Foucault emphasizes a sharp break that separates the modern period from the premodern. In the premodern period, punishment usually took the form of public physical punishment and death—principally, brutal torture and public hangings—such as Foucault graphically describes in the brutal opening of *Discipline and Punish* (1979, 3–6). But later, in the eighteenth century, reformers began turning against punishment aimed at the criminal's body; instead, they called for a "gentle way in punishment" (104), which was aimed at his mind or soul. The reformers argued that the criminal is also a human being with a mind, and thus he should be treated in a rational way, rather than beaten like an animal. While some argued that this more rational treatment would be more humane, it would also be more efficient in curing crime. By the middle of the nineteenth century, the reformers' modern approach to the criminal was generally accepted, and physical punishment was replaced by a prison system which still exists. Since this modern prison system seems far more humane than the brutal punishment which it replaced, modernists have tended to regard this history as a story of progress, a history which shows that reason is gradually taking us toward a better world. Foucault's postmodern analysis is far more complicated and far more pessimistic about what reason can do for us.

In developing his analysis Foucault centers on Jeremy Bentham's *Panopticon* (Foucault 1979, e.g., 135–36, 152–53, 157), a late-eighteenth-century book which advocated the reformer's modern approach to criminals and which was to be a major influence on punitive reasoning throughout the nineteenth and twentieth centuries. It is also a book which gives us a terrifying description of the model prison of the future. In this prison everything will be under the control of the warden-overseer, with the prisoners placed in isolated individual cells. The warden-overseer will sit in a central observation tower from which he can look into each of the brightly lit cells encircling his tower. While he can see the prisoners—perhaps we should think of him as the omnipotent "eye of reason"—they won't be able to see him. Consequently, they will be forced to live with the thought, "Is he now looking at me?" And since they cannot know the answer, they will start acting as if the Rational Eye is always looking at them.

According to the new theory, the constant pressure from a normal, rational eye will eventually cause criminals to give up their deviant ways and become normal. The reformers were right in saying that the criminal's soul should be cured, and it can be cured—not through brutal punishment, but by means of a more rational approach to deviant behavior. In Bentham's *Panopticon*, this more rational approach becomes incarceration with constant surveillance by an expert.

In centering on Bentham's panopticon Foucault emphasizes not the absence of physical punishment but the new presence of a social institution which has total power over an inmate's soul. In the premodern era of punitive reason the prison played only a minor role and was seen as a place where criminals were sent to remove them from society, but in the modern period the prison becomes a place where the criminal soul will be constantly assaulted by overwhelming force. What is thus important is that the panopticon represents a much more pervasive and powerful system for controlling deviance and individual freedom. In other words, what is important is a new system of dominance. It is a system which is always in close contact with the deviant's soul, and unlike the premodern system, which left the soul alone and was controlled only by the authority of a distant king, it is almost impossible to escape from.

Foucault also stresses that in this panoptical system the key to dominance is constant surveillance by experts who judge and act in the name of the "social norm" rather than in the name of the king or our ancestors. These modern experts in punitive reason think of crime not as a display of animal passion, but rather as a "sickness" of the soul that must be treated and prevented from spreading into the social body. In order to cure it, the experts must look closely at the deviant's soul, and so they began the systematic accumulation of a great deal of knowledge about deviancy, giving birth to the "social sciences." As in medicine, treatment required examinations, and so the deviant and potential deviant must be subjected to a great many of them. The "rational eye" continues to look down from the tower, only now seeming much closer, carefully checking to see whether or not you are upholding the "norm."

What Foucault argues at the end of *Discipline* is that panoptical punitive reasoning produced a system of dominance which eventually moved beyond the prison and became the main technique for controlling deviance in modern Western societies. This happened gradually in the nineteenth and twentieth centuries as the new system—with its constant surveillance, professional knowledge, experts in the "norm," and examinations—spread to Western schools, workhouses, and factories. In spreading out, the new system created a disciplinary society with "complete and austere institutions" (1979, 231) in harmony with the demands of rational and industrialized profit making. More recently, the system has been strengthened by television cameras, computers, and data banks, so that today we can keep a close "rational eye" on just about everything that moves.

Here it should be emphasized that Foucault is not arguing that the eighteenth-century reformers *wanted* to create a disciplinary prison system or society—they simply wanted to produce more humane and efficient treatment of criminals. And they certainly would not have wanted what has today become obvious: a system of incarceration that breeds rather than cures crime. What happened is what also happened with Luther and Calvin, who did not want to create the most materialistic society in world history. In both cases, the reformers' descriptions of the world set in motion a cultural development that had unintended consequences as a result of other historical developments.

In discussing these developments Foucault argues that as soon as the new prison system was adopted, many could see that it was creating a permanent class of criminals, but he also argues that curing actual criminals wasn't its main purpose anyway: the main purpose was to establish some clear definitions of a type of crime that had only recently taken on great importance, crime against property. The definitions were needed because at the time French society was in transition from a feudal society, in which property was not the key to value, to a capitalist society, in which property was everything.

There was a problem because, with the end of the old regime, a great many peasants and poor workers were suddenly on the move throughout the countryside and towns, and they just didn't respect property. They were doing all sorts of things that showed their disrespect—breaking their employer's machines, stealing from him, and even organizing themselves into unions despite laws against doing so! A large part of the problem, as viewed by the more privileged members of the emerging capitalist society, was that many of the peasants and members of the working classes didn't regard their crimes against property as "crime." Who could have a deep respect for the law after God's king was guillotined? Everybody now knew that there was nothing behind the law but the rich. And what if the lawless bad attitude of these emerging poor workers were to spread to the rest of the population? Where would the new capitalist order be then?

According to Foucault, this dangerous historical situation produced a generalized social fear, and it was this fear that encouraged acceptance of the new prison system. Crimes against property had to be clearly defined, and a new system of incarceration might be just the thing to make things clear. And when it also became clear that the new system was producing a new class of permanent delinquents, so what? The main thing was to let the majority know what happens to anyone who messes with property. It also turned out that the creation of a permanent delinquent class wasn't bad for *everybody*, for it diverted attention from the profit making of the privileged classes. The fear of an increase in delinquency also explains why the disciplinary system was allowed to spread to schools, factories, and the rest of society. It also helps to explain why a new caste of experts was soon busy suppressing individual freedom all over town. And Foucault's discussion of how modern human beings were willing to surrender their freedom in the name of the "norm" is perhaps the most interesting part of his book.

With the takeover by modern punitive reason, the number of literal prisons has increased to an unimaginable degree. Whether the entire system will be able to survive today's enormous prison expenditures remains to be seen—perhaps it can even survive California's "three strikes and you're out" policy. But at present there is no strong movement toward an alternative system that might control deviance without producing a permanent and expensive class of self-hating and unloving Others.

What is Foucault trying to show us in his postmodern history of punitive reason? First, modern human beings are not discovering the truth about madness or criminals or anything else; through their changing descriptions of the world, they are simply producing new kinds of worlds to live in. Rather than truth, modern reason and knowledge serve a will to power, as Nietzsche and Heidegger said; and since knowledge-claims are always tied to power, Foucault thinks we should be specific and talk about "power-knowledge relations" (1979, 27). He especially wants us to see that despite many experts, textbooks, and scientific thinkers, there is nothing especially objective about the descriptive languages of modern experts—including those of lawyers, sociologists, psychologists, and teachers. These languages also have roots in the desires of some people to dominate others. As Foucault says:

> Perhaps, too, we should abandon a whole tradition that allows us
> to imagine that knowledge can exist only where the power relations
> are suspended and that knowledge can develop only outside its in-
> junctions, its demands, and its interests. Perhaps we should aban-
> don the belief that power makes mad and that, by the same token,
> the renunciation of power is one of the conditions of knowledge.
> We should admit rather that power produces knowledge . . . ; that
> power and knowledge directly imply one another; that there is no
> power relation without the correlative constitution of a field of
> knowledge, nor any knowledge that does not presuppose and con-
> stitute at the same time power relations. (1979, 27)

Foucault also wants us to see that the acceptance of the languages of modern experts has been influenced by specific historical developments, thus reminding us that a new way of describing the world is not the whole story. Like Rorty, Weber, and Marx, he shows us that nonlinguistic historical developments are also important, but unlike Marx, he doesn't try to reduce those developments to changing economic conditions. Foucault also wants us to see something terrible: that although the Other has changed throughout history, the process of producing the Other has remained—specifically, that the new, more rational language that appeared after the seventeenth century produced a new delinquent class of Other. And to make the story worse, Foucault wants us to see that the creation of the new Untouchable—like the new disciplinary society in which everyone learned to respect and guard property—especially served the interests of the few who have privilege and power.

Finally, Foucault emphasizes that with the development of a more rational, disciplinary society, human beings have lost a great deal of freedom. Like Max Weber, Foucault equates the advance of reason with a smaller and smaller cage for the individual. It is a cage in which there is little room for play, the imagination, or individual freedom.

To summarize this brief postmodern story about the social history of human beings: for Geertz, it began more than a million years ago with the gradual emergence of a language-using animal that lost its instincts—a new kind of incomplete creature who had a desperate need for language and other systems of symbols to tell it what to think, feel, and do in the world. Because of its great incompleteness, this new creature was capable of believing and desiring almost anything, and thus it has a history. In this history, in response to a multitude of causes, the creature keeps changing itself and its world through redescriptions that catch on. If Weber is right, the story changed greatly in the modern period as a result of some sixteenth- and seventeenth-century Protestant redescriptions which, after mingling with Western rationalism, eventually gave rise to the secularized, well-developed capitalist societies in the Western world. What happened was that the incomplete "hero" began to play a new part, that of a rational moneymaker, and as a result he became fabulously wealthy.

But, unfortunately, money doesn't solve all problems, and two in particular dominate the modern story: first, the rational approach to life that created wealth also created increasingly narrow and boring work cages, and, as Foucault says, to fit us into these cages, it has also created a disciplinary society in which everybody has a constant eye on the Other, looking for any trace of a free individual who exists outside of the rational "norm."

Today this problem of an oppressive rational world seems interconnected with another major problem that has dominated the social life of the incomplete animal—the problem of the Other. This problem seems to have its deepest roots in what gave us our history in the first place—our incomplete nature and desperate need for language. For as the species gave itself up to a social organization based on language, it began living in a new kind of world—a world which is filled not only with the positive but also the negative, not only with "us" and "superiors" but also "them" and "inferiors." What Foucault shows us is that this problem will not be solved with a more rational language. As we have seen in earlier chapters, the postmodern hopeful think that the solution lies in a more imaginative language—one which teaches the incomplete hero to take pleasure in the Other, who exists outside the cage.

6 Postmodernism and Multiculturalism

The topic of postmodernism often comes up in discussions of multiculturalism, so in this chapter we will focus on how postmodern thought relates to the current debate over multiculturalism in American education. If a teacher took seriously the view outlined in this book—in particular, the postmodern ideas about truth, reason, language, the self, the Other, power, creativity, and the aesthetic—how might it influence her thinking about a multicultural approach to education?

In dealing with this question, we should first note that the multicultural movement developed out of the charge that American education has focused too narrowly on the dominant Euramerican culture and history, excluding the Others. Pointing out that American society includes people from many different cultures, multiculturalists argue that there is a need to move beyond traditional Eurocentric arrogance and think about the rest of the world. Feminists have also pointed out that there is more to culture and history than the "dead-white-male" story.

To some extent this movement in favor of a broader approach to American education began at the turn of the century with the creation of the separate discipline of anthropology. From its inception American anthropology has focused primarily on non-European cultures, and it has consistently put down ethnocentrism and attempted to picture the Other as our equal. Here the names of Boas, Benedict, and Mead immediately come to mind, and they and other anthropologists have undoubtedly had a major liberating influence on American education. But what many of today's multiculturalists argue is that we need to go much further than simply glancing at a few nonliterate societies, and to a large extent the debate is over how far an educator should go in singling out and praising the diverse groups that make up American society.

In arguing for a more multicultural education, multiculturalists often emphasize that in a society and world filled with widespread cultural diversity, successful communication and the avoidance of conflict require a sensitivity to diversity. It is also argued that one of the reasons students from Other groups do poorly in American classrooms is that their teachers don't know them. Multiculturalists sometimes point to two other problems resulting from a narrow Eurocentric education. First, it makes students from European backgrounds feel superior. If it was *our* ancestors who created everything that is worth studying, then *we* belong at the top today. On the other hand, such an education makes the non-European Other feel inferior. If we learn that *our* ancestors did nothing worth studying, then *we* must belong at the bottom. Although such inferences may not be rational, and perhaps not consciously thought out, it is easy to imagine them—and a more multicultural approach to education is needed to prevent them. As Charles Taylor reminds us in his essay in *Multiculturalism*, a human identity is "dialogical" (1994, 33), i.e., built upon how others recognize people like "us." Multicultural education is an attempt to gain positive recognition for Others.

In responding to such arguments, a postmodern would be especially sensitive to the need for an education that includes the Other, and the multicultural movement has been greatly influenced by postmodern ideas on the topic. In this book, we have emphasized that postmoderns tend to place the relation between "us" and "them" at the center of our social and psychological lives. We have also discussed Rorty's suggestion that cruel treatment of the Other is the major moral problem faced by human societies. Whether this cruelty is a result of the belief that the Other is inferior or simply a result of insensitivity and a lack of curiosity about him, from a postmodern point of view, it is the consistently ugly part of the human story.

Part of the solution is thus an education that focuses not only on the Other, but also on why the Other has been a persistent problem in human societies. Here we might think of stories and books like Wright's "Big Boy Leaves Home," Kosinski's *The Painted Bird*, and Foucault's *Discipline and Punish*. As these works illustrate, such an Other-centered education would focus not only on the fear of difference, but also on the complex need which explains why the Other has continued to play a major role in human history. In other words, what is needed is an education which doesn't turn away from the terrible part of the human story. To show the rest of the story, what is also needed is an education which shows students the value of the sublime. Here, as in the art of Picasso's weeping women paintings, students experience the pleasure of moving outside their rational cages of sameness, the sublime pleasure of playing with the Other.

A postmodern would also support the multicultural argument that the standard Eurocentric bias in American education tends to make kids from European backgrounds feel superior, while making non-European kids feel inferior. If Saussure, Wittgenstein, Geertz, and Rorty are right in claiming that public descriptions shape how individuals come to think about themselves, and if the language of American education raises the European story above that of the Others, white self-esteem will also be raised above that of the Others. This seems hard to deny, but there is more to it than the actual curriculum of American education; it also involves the worshipful way the "Great White Story" has been presented. In other words, teachers need to point out that Classical Greece means more than Plato and the Parthenon—it also means misogyny and slavery.

Yet, it is a mistake to think that the self-esteem problem involves only an ethnocentric presentation of Western civilization in American classrooms; it is also related to thoughts about who has the money and power, "us" or "them." While postmoderns don't have to take a Nietzschean line that power is everything, they cannot ignore that it plays a major role in shaping an individual's self-esteem. What should not be forgotten is that it is terribly normal for human beings to associate power with superiority and weakness with inferiority. Consequently, a positive presentation of the cultures and histories of a non-European group—say, the Aztecs—will not necessarily increase an Indian student's pride in his group and self, since the bitter fact is that the Europeans won the fight. How many students can resist the kind of thinking that led the powerless boy in *The Painted Bird* to conclude that his powerful oppressor is God, and that people like himself are less than human? This is not an argument in favor of such thinking; nor is it an argument against a multicultural education—which we need—but it casts doubt on the assumption that merely by studying Other cultures we will overcome white arrogance and the low self-esteem of the non-European Other.

One problem with many self-esteem arguments—which have been uncritically run to death in American education during the past few years—is that they have tended to ignore the importance of power. The basic idea, that self-confidence is important when struggling to overcome life's difficulties, is sound. But what is needed, say, when a student starts getting low grades during the first year of college, is the "confidence" that by working hard he can control the future through his own efforts. It should also be noted that this kind of confidence can coexist with a great deal of self-hatred—the same self-hatred which drives the behavior of many high-achieving personalities. The point here isn't that self-hatred is good, but that by itself it does not prevent the self-discipline and delay of gratification necessary for achievement. What does— in other words, what explains the apathetic and low-achieving personalities that Malcolm X was fighting in the ghettos—is the individual's feeling that no matter how hard he works, he cannot master his future.

This is the problem that Keynes understood in revising laissez-faire economic theory to meet the demands of the Great Depression. Specifically, Keynes understood that through inductive reasoning, people will tend to assume that a prolonged depression will continue into the future, and as a result, they won't make the investments that foster the economic activity needed to end a depression. The reason Keynes advocated expenditures by the federal government—"pumping money into the economy"—was to overcome such depression reasoning and get people to once again invest and sacrifice for a better future. The problem for teachers of ghetto students is also how to create such hope, and it seems obvious that telling positive stories about a student's ancestors isn't nearly enough. In dealing with this problem many years ago Harlem psychologist Kenneth Clark argued that the key was "demonstrable achievement." In other words, teachers who want to raise a student's self-esteem should arrange their classes so that the student can see that he is capable of mastering difficult subject matter. Self-esteem based on anything else seems insignificant.

But here teachers shouldn't kid themselves: no matter what we do in the classroom, as long as the dominant majority allows America's ghettos and housing projects to exist in their present form, there will also exist a great many disorganized and nonachieving ghetto personalities—personalities which will eventually fill America's many prisons. Low self-esteem helps to explain the lives of people trapped in ghetto environments, but ghettos are more than low self-esteem. They are places which are filled with fatalism, disorganized and fatherless families, and self-destructive and alienated peer groups, as well as places where the prevailing cultural tradition does not place a high value on education. But by now surely the dominant majority has a sense of what an America's ghettos are like; and let's hope Foucault is wrong when he says that such a situation—which has long been America's disgrace—exists because the dominant majority feels a need for a permanent Other. The popularity of the recent talk about IQ inferiority can only make us wonder.

But to return to multiculturalism, after working with hundreds of educators in Los Angeles and many other cities during the past few years, as well as collaborating with organizations such as the Los Angeles Educational Partnership, CHART (Rockefeller Foundation), and the Panasonic Foundation, we have found that a great many teachers are concerned with sensitizing their students to cultural differences and the value of the Other. Specifically, American teachers are now dealing regularly with topics such as prejudice, race, gender, the media's presentation of the Other, color symbolism, and the need for a multiracial standard of beauty. These teachers are not just defending the status quo, and many are now using humanities and literature books which deal with nondominant cultures.

On the other hand, many teachers are not sure of what they should say about the non-European cultures. Should they be honest and point out cases of sexism, clitoridectomies, color prejudice, undemocratic authoritarianism and stagnant traditionalism, and cruelty toward the Other? This issue is connected with the issue of whether teachers should encourage students from a nondominant culture to hang on to it. Would such a student be better off sticking with her "roots," rather than attempting to fit into the American "mainstream"? All cultural backgrounds are mixtures of positive and negative elements, and simpleminded assimilation into the mainstream is obviously not the answer— but what is? In dealing with these issues, teachers who want to continue living in democratic societies should not ignore the need for a democratic society to harmonize the diverse interests of different groups. But aside from this crucial problem, what should a postmodern teacher say about hanging on to nondominant traditions, assuming that the teacher's goal is empowerment and equalizing life chances in a democratic society?

While there is no single "postmodern answer" to these questions, several things should be kept in mind in approaching them. To begin with, we should not forget that for students cultures come as wholes; we should also keep in mind that all cultures are mixtures of strengths and weaknesses. Thus, when we tell a student to hang on to a culture, he will not hang on only to its strengths.

Postmodern pragmatists will also keep in mind that an internalized culture is not like a light cloak which sits on top of a self-sufficient human nature with built-in thoughts, feelings, and behavioral patterns. Rather, as Geertz shows in *The Interpretation of Cultures,* an internalized culture is a system of symbols which dominates everything in an incomplete animal's life, shaping not only her beliefs, emotions, and values, but also her goals and the ways in which she attempts to realize them. Furthermore, teachers should not forget that human beings are typically engaged in power struggles, or that people from some cultures cannot compete on an equal footing with people from other cultures. As has been emphasized throughout this book, postmoderns tend to assume that the most important differences between human beings are a result of the cultures which have formed them. It follows that all cultures are not equal when it comes to power. What also seems clear is that students from cultures that place a high value on reason, literacy, science, democracy, and economic rationality have been the most successful.

With regard to literacy, a major weakness in some cultures is that they don't place a high value on reading, writing, and formal education. While "major weakness" might seem too strong a term here, many writers have recently argued that literacy must be seen as a tool of enormous social power, and thus the brief digression which follows.

During the past few years, several major works have been written on the impact of literacy, e.g., Havelock's *Preface to Plato;* Goody's *The Domestication of the Savage Mind;* Ong's *Orality and Literacy;* Todorov's *The Conquest of America;* and Olson's *The World on Paper.* In these books the authors argue that in giving rise to cultures based on books, the alphabet didn't just change the way human beings communicate and store information; it also changed the way they think and act in the world.

In relation to social power, Todorov's *The Conquest of America* is especially important because it argues that Cortés and the Europeans were able to defeat Montezuma and the Indians because of superior communication skills. For Todorov, these skills are grounded in a writing-based culture, and they include getting accurate information quickly (about what the Other is like), interpreting it realistically (as information about human beings in *this* world, rather than about what the gods have in mind), and using the information in a manipulative way (through dissimulation and outright lying) in order to dominate the Other. Literate Cortés was quick to find out what the Indians were like, where they were divided, and that they had a Quetzalcoatl myth; and (while pretending to be God, telling the Indians that he was getting supernatural signs on his compass and even that he was carrying on a conversation with his horse!) he became one of history's biggest and most successful liars, before the development of American advertising.

On the other hand, illiterate Montezuma was slow to figure out what the Spaniards were up to, interpreting the information he gathered as a sign of what the gods had in mind rather than of what the Spaniards had in mind. Montezuma also failed to control what the Indians thought about Cortés, helping Cortés to create the impression that God had landed, thus crippling the Indian desire to fight until it was too late. The end result was that several hundred Europeans with their recently gathered Indian allies were able to destroy a military society that fielded tens of thousands of experienced warriors. This isn't the place to discuss Todorov's full argument, but it is important to emphasize his point that when the Other meets the Other, communication skills are crucial if there is to be a struggle for dominance. What is even more important is Todorov's striking claim that writing was the key to Cortés's superiority at communication. (Here it should be noted that the Aztecs had only a rudimentary writing system of a few pictograms, while the Europeans had a book culture that stretched back to the development of a phonetic alphabet around 750 years B.C.E.)

A reader of Diaz's eyewitness account of *The Conquest of the New Spain* will have no doubt about Cortés's superiority at gaining information and using it to dominate the Other. But the interesting question is why this superiority is related to writing. Here we might briefly look at Havelock's *Preface to Plato,* which argues that it was the invention of the Greek alphabet and a literate culture which made fifth-century philosophy possible. Havelock specifically argues that in the *Iliad* and the *Odyssey,* which were written down shortly after the Greeks had invented their alphabet, there is still no trace of philosophical or scientific thinking. In particular, there is a lack of abstract distinctions, analysis, and subtle psychological probing, and there is no celebration of human reason (beyond Odysseus's cleverness). For Havelock, Homer's worldview is typical of that found in oral-based cultures. In such a culture the mind is inevitably preoccupied with conservative memory work—with hanging on to community beliefs that are essential to the survival of a cultural group—and this restricts the development of abstract categories and analytical thought. Only in a writing-based culture is a mind freed for such thought. As Roger Brown has pointed out in *Words and Things,* early languages contained few highly abstract categories such as "one," "order," "quality" and "organism." Here there are two points that should be emphasized: first, written records free the mind from memory work and, second, they make words visible as words—i.e., as arbitrary signs that stand out on a lifeless page and can then be analyzed. Once the mind is freed for analysis, and once words are recognized as words, science, philosophy, and psychology can move beyond the simplistic thinking found in Homer.

Furthermore, once words appear on a page, it becomes possible to think about knowledge in a new way—as what follows reasonably from evidence that is actively gathered and critically examined. In a writing-based culture, it isn't authority and tradition that make a belief true, but rather the evidence gathered in support of it. This postliterate way of thinking about knowledge is important not because it leads to truth, but because it turns human beings into aggressive pursuers of what Foucault calls "knowledge-power."

In *In My Father's House: Africa in the Philosophy of Culture,* Kwame Appiah discusses the intellectual history of Africa, and he supports the claim that people from oral backgrounds think of knowledge as what has already been passed down from ancestors. People from oral cultures did, of course, think that some human beings knew more than others, and also that there were practical things that needed to be found out, but they regarded theoretical knowledge as rooted in tradition and authority. This separates them from people who grow up under writing-based cultures and who think of knowledge as constantly growing out of hard-won evidence, the avoidance of inconsistency, and precise reasoning (1992, 130–34). There was no problem as long as people from oral societies were living in a traditional world, or, as Nietzsche might put it, as long as they were facing oral savages, but they were crippled when they came up against literate savages. Nor has this situation changed at the end of the twentieth century.

The claim that literacy changes how human beings think about the world is substantiated by A. R. Luria's studies of illiterate Russian peasants during the 1930s (as discussed in Ong 1982, 49–56). In particular, Luria found that illiterates were poor at classifying objects in abstract categories. For example, they had trouble classifying an ax with other "tools" such as a hammer and a saw, and instead lumped it together with a tree, since axes are used to chop down trees. Like Homer, they were more likely to think in terms of concrete situations than in terms of abstract categories. Luria also demonstrated that illiterates were slow at coming up with descriptions of themselves as individuals, and also that they were poor at syllogistic, formal reasoning—e.g., they had difficulty answering the following question: "If all bears in the far North are white, and the polar bear lives in the far North, what is its color?" Luria's point isn't that the illiterate peasants lacked the innate capacity to answer this question, form abstract classifications, and describe themselves, but that because they came from an oral culture, they lacked the inclination to perform such mental operations. Such people are no match for the Cortéses of the world.

The main point is that people from cultures which do not place a high value on reading and writing will not be able to compete with people from cultures which do. The Aztecs who preached that "words are for women, weapons are for men" did not realize that, as Richard Wright said four centuries later, "words are weapons," and thus they were defeated. Todorov makes us realize that even if a writing-based culture wasn't the immediate cause of Cortés's victory in Mexico (other causes often cited include the divisions among the Indians, their lack of resistance to European diseases, and Montezuma's indecisiveness), it guaranteed that eventually the Spaniards would have won. Perhaps anthropologist Lévi-Strauss overstates the point when he says that "the primary function of writing, as a means of communication, is to facilitate the enslavement of other human beings" (1961, 291–92), but multiculturalists should not ignore that power struggles are likely to continue in the world and that those who do not value reading and writing will lose. Nor should it be forgotten that people who cannot control their world end up hating themselves, like the boy in *The Painted Bird*. What eventually changed the boy and gave him self-confidence at the end of the book wasn't exposure to ancestral worship but the ability to define the world in his way. For this reason classrooms devoted to the former should not be promoted at the expense of classrooms devoted to books and academic achievement.

Throughout this book we have focused on another aspect of the modern tradition which accompanied the development of literacy in the West, the celebration of reason as the key to the good life. We have seen that postmoderns such as Foucault and Lyotard have criticized this idea because the goal of a more rational social life has often resulted in terror and the exclusion of the Other. But, as is illustrated through a contrast with traditional societies that ignored reason and continued to follow ancestors, traditions, and priests, reason is not without value. In other words, from the postmodern thought that "reason excludes," we don't need to conclude that we should stop reasoning! This may seem obvious, but in today's multicultural debates we sometimes hear people automatically put down a reasoned defense of a position (often dismissed under the heading of "linear thinking"), as though reasoning were at the root of all evil. For the pragmatic postmodern, it is not; and although we don't need Le Corbusier's International Style of life, we do need architects and engineers who are good at reasoning. In other words, reason and a concern with precise distinctions and logical development should be regarded not as evil but as a tool which is useful for some purposes but not for others.

Teachers should also be clear about the alternatives to reason as a guide to the good life. Only the linguistic imagination has been praised in this book, and we should not forget that tradition-bound, authority-loving, and passionate societies have also persecuted and eliminated the Other. As Martha Nussbaum points out in "Feminists and Philosophy," women did not do well in societies which were guided by tradition. It should also be noted that although Cortés's society placed a higher value on reason, it wasn't the only society which was willing to sacrifice human beings. Finally, while postmoderns assume that reason is, like everything else, tied to a will to remake the world, this doesn't establish that it is inevitably tied to dominance over other human beings.

In short, postmodern teachers shouldn't say that reason—with its urge to replace the particular and the doubtful with the universal and the certain—is *always* a problem; the problem is an excessive reliance on reason and the belief that reason will take us to truth. For example, in criticizing Kant's rationalistic ethics, Rorty isn't saying that we should stop reasoning about what we're doing wrong; what he is saying is that reasoning isn't enough, and that in order to bring about human solidarity and a reduction of cruelty, it must be supplemented with imaginative linguistic redescriptions of the world. Multiculturalists should also keep in mind that societies without rational technology have done poorly in the twentieth century; some have not even been able to feed themselves.

This leads us to the question of economic behavior. Here postmoderns disagree, but given the failure of communism in the Soviet Union and Eastern Europe, it looks as though, for all of their flaws, capitalist societies with mixed economies will continue to prevail in the world (with luck, they'll also be arranged to provide for the welfare of all). And if they do continue, people from cultures which do not foster economic rationality—think of diligence, frugality, prudence, punctuality, and a willingness to go by the terms of one's contract—will not be able to compete with people who come from cultures which do. Perhaps one of the main weaknesses in postmodern thought is that it too often reduces everything to power struggles and dominance, leaving economics in the background. But one doesn't have to be a Marxist to realize that production is also enormously important. As Thomas Sowell has emphasized in *Race and Economics,* in our postmodern era politics has sometimes become a substitute for production:

> In societies or among groups without skills required for economic productivity and economic organization, politics is, if not "the only game in town," then at least one of the few games for which players have the necessary skills. As the main focus of talents and ambitions, politics can readily become both intricate and desperate. Preoccupation with politics may become a *substitute* for productivity, for either individuals or groups. An Idi Amin or an Adolf Hitler could hardly expect to acquire enough economic skills to rise from unpromising beginnings to anything resembling the prominence they achieved in politics. Groups or nations that are generations behind others in economic skills may also seek political shortcuts to importance, whether through ideology, symbolism, confiscations, terrorism, or war. (1994, 148)

Sowell also points out that in the face of racist and ethnic power relations, groups which have become productive—e.g., the Japanese—have done well at combating Western prejudice and an inferior position in the world. They have done well as a consequence of having cultures which encourage economic rationality and productivity, and not merely because of political activity.

Sowell makes the additional point that when we encourage people from nondominant backgrounds to place a high value on their traditional identities, we also encourage them to think that it's "treason" (1994, 30) to copy the dominant culture. This is especially the case if the dominant group is pictured as hostile to the advancement of outsiders. But as Sowell points out, throughout history the copying of a dominant culture has paid off not only in terms of a higher standard of living, but also in terms of power. The Americans who stole and copied British industrial designs helped the United States economically as well as politically, and the Japanese who began copying American cars are not suffering because of it. Today they are also developing their own, just as Europeans were soon developing the Arab science that they began copying at the beginning of the modern era. In brief, by encouraging people from nondominant backgrounds to "stick with their own," multiculturalists can block their chances for economic advancement; and without such advancement it is difficult to see how the powerless can gain power. This point is hard to argue against in a market-based world which is without a workable alternative, and yet some multiculturalists talk as though the only problem is what the Others must "give up" if they copy a culture that is economically successful.

Sowell reminds us of what seems obvious: that all cultures are not equal when it comes to producing economic rationality and goods and services, just as they are not equal when it comes to producing precise reasoners and highly literate critical thinkers. Yet it is surprising how often this is overlooked or downplayed in multicultural talk that focuses only on the oppressive side of the Eurocentric tradition. Perhaps such unwillingness to talk about any kind of cultural inequality is partially a consequence of the postmodern rejection of truth, for it is easy to infer from "no culture knows the truth" that "all cultures are equal." In teaching postmodernism we have noticed that some students at first draw this inference, but it is a mistake, and it should be pointed out. Specifically, we should not let our students think that Nazi culture in 1935 was equal to American culture in 1935, and we should not let them think that either ghetto gang culture or macho militia culture in 1996 is equal to mainstream middle-class American culture in 1996. Rather than self-destructive relativism, we should tell them not only that some cultures work better than others, but also that some are morally superior to others because they strive to avoid cruelty, and, as Judith Shklar says, "cruelty is the worst thing [we] do" (1984, 43–44).

So what should be the main goal of a postmodern approach to multiculturalism? First, it should not be to produce a nation of mindless copiers. As Vonnegut says in *Breakfast of Champions*, there is a great deal of trash and ugliness in the dominant culture that should be thrown out rather than copied, and this is also the case in nondominant cultures.

Some things shouldn't be copied because they are cruel, and others shouldn't be copied because they don't work.

But at this point notice how easy it is for a postmodern to say that since no culture has the truth, Americans should simply worry about what works in a democratic society. This is the same shift that was advocated by some American thinkers at the end of the nineteenth century; faced with a democratic society filled with great cultural diversity—a society in which several immigrant groups thought that they alone had the truth—these thinkers developed a new, American approach to philosophy called "pragmatism." In this new philosophy, especially as developed by William James and John Dewey, Americans were told to forget about who had the truth, because there wasn't any. For James, as for Dewey, the only sensible alternative was to focus on "what is good in the way of belief" (1978, 42), i.e., on ideas that will make a better future. In reviving pragmatism for an even more diverse America in the 1980s and 1990s, Richard Rorty coupled James's advice with a postmodern view of the world, and Rorty's synthesis has been a major influence on this book. Part of the value of such pragmatic advice is that it encourages all groups, including the dominant group, to downplay the importance of the cultures and ethnic identities which separate them—and this is what makes a pluralistic and democratic society possible.

The postmodern idea that there is no truth might at first seem demoralizing, especially for those who feel insecure about playing around in an insubstantial pageant, but it is also liberating. Not only are we liberated from the burden of searching for what cannot be found, we are also liberated from an oppressive urge to shove others and ourselves into our preconceived cages. This postmodern liberation is important because it redirects our energy toward what human beings are good at—creating ourselves and the worlds we live in. It is important because it opens up the possibility of creating new kinds of identities and social relationships, which, unlike those of the past, are not brought into existence against the Other. What we need to remember is that it is our linguistic imagination that makes possible such creations; and in trying to recreate ourselves and our world, we would do well to keep in mind the problem of the Other, the importance of reducing cruelty, the question of what will work politically and economically, and, of course, the importance of a good play.

Works Cited

Aaron, Daniel, moderator. 1966. "Thirty Years Later: Memories of the First American Writers' Congress." *American Scholar* 35: 495–516.

Allen, Barry. 1993. *Truth in Philosophy.* Cambridge, MA: Harvard University Press.

Appiah, Kwame Anthony. 1992. *In My Father's House: Africa in the Philosophy of Culture.* New York: Oxford University Press.

Auerbach, Erich. 1953. *Mimesis: The Representation of Reality in Western Literature.* Translated by Willard R. Trask. Princeton, NJ: Princeton University Press.

Barthes, Roland. 1992. "The Death of the Author." In *Modern Literary Theory: A Reader,* 2nd ed., edited by Philip Rice and Patricia Waugh, 114–27. London: Edward Arnold.

Baudrillard, Jean. 1988. *Selected Writings.* Edited by Mark Poster. Cambridge, MA: Polity.

Bauman, Zygmut. 1992. *Intimations of Postmodernity.* New York: Routledge.

Beardsley, Monroe C. 1966. *Aesthetics from Classical Greece to the Present: A Short History.* New York: Macmillan.

Beckett, Samuel. 1982. *Waiting for Godot: Tragicomedy in 2 Acts.* New York: Grove.

Bentham, Jeremy. 1995. *The Panopticon Writings.* New York: Verso.

Berger, John, et al. 1972. *Ways of Seeing: A Book Made by John Berger (and Others).* Harmondsworth: British Broadcasting Company and Penguin Books.

Brown, Roger W. 1968. *Words and Things.* New York: Free Press.

Burke, Kenneth. 1968. "Interaction: III. Dramatism." In *International Encyclopedia of the Social Sciences,* vol. 7, edited by David L. Sills, 445–52. New York: Macmillan.

Burkert, Walter, René Girard, and Jonathan Z. Smith. 1987. *Violent Origins: On Ritual Killing and Cultural Formation.* Edited by Robert G. Hamerton-Kelly. Stanford, CA: Stanford University Press.

Canaday, John. 1959. *Mainstreams of Modern Art.* New York: Henry Holt.

Cronenberg, David, dir. 1982. *Videodrome.* Film. 90 min. Universal City, CA: Universal Studios.

Crowley, Sharon. 1989. *A Teacher's Introduction to Deconstruction.* Urbana, IL: National Council of Teachers of English.

Crusius, Timothy W. 1991. *A Teacher's Introduction to Philosophical Hermeneutics.* Urbana, IL: National Council of Teachers of English.

Culler, Jonathan. 1977. *Ferdinand de Saussure.* New York: Penguin.

Danto, Arthur C. 1965. *Nietzsche as Philosopher.* New York: Macmillan.

Darwin, Charles. 1964. *On the Origin of Species.* Facsim. ed. Cambridge, MA: Harvard University Press.

Derrida, Jacques. 1973. *Speech and Phenomena and Other Essays on Husserl's Theory of Signs.* Translated by David Allison. Evanston, IL: Northwestern University Press.

———. 1976. *Of Grammatology.* Translated by Gayatri Chakravorty Spivak. Baltimore: Johns Hopkins University Press.

———. 1978. *Writing and Difference.* Translated by Alan Bass. London: Routledge & Kegan Paul.

———. 1981. *Margins of Philosophy.* Translated by Alan Bass. Chicago: Chicago University Press.

———. 1989. "Structure, Sign and Play in the Discourse of the Human Sciences." In *Modern Literary Theory: A Reader,* edited by Philip Rice and Patricia Waugh, 149–165. London: Edward Arnold.

Descartes, René. 1969. *The Essential Descartes.* Edited by Margaret D. Wilson. New York: New American Library.

Diaz, Bernal. 1963. *The Conquest of New Spain.* Translated by J. M. Cohen. New York: Penguin.

Docherty, Thomas, ed. 1993. *Postmodernism: A Reader.* New York: Columbia University Press.

Dreyfus, Hubert L. 1991. *Being-in-the-World: A Commentary on Heidegger's "Being and Time," Division I.* Cambridge, MA: MIT Press.

Eco, Umberto, with Richard Rorty, Jonathan Culler, and Christine Brooke-Rose. 1992. *Interpretation and Overinterpretation.* Edited by Stefan Collini. New York: Cambridge University Press.

Ellison, Ralph. 1989. *Invisible Man.* New York: Vintage.

Feenberg, Andrew. 1995. *Alternative Modernity: The Technical Turn in Philosophy and Social Theory.* Berkeley: University of California Press.

Flaubert, Gustav. 1958. *Madame Bovary.* New York: Pocket Books.

Foucault, Michel. 1965. *Madness and Civilization: A History of Insanity in the Age of Reason.* Translated by Richard Howard. New York: Vintage.

———. 1979. *Discipline and Punish: The Birth of the Prison.* Translated by Alan Sheridan. New York: Vintage.

Freud, Sigmund. 1930. *Civilization and Its Discontents.* Translated by Joan Riviere. London: Hogarth.

Gardner, Helen D. 1970. *Gardner's Art through the Ages.* 5th ed. Revised by Horst de la Croix and Richard G. Tansey. New York: Harcourt, Brace.

Garver, Newton. 1994. *This Complicated Form of Life: Essays on Wittgenstein.* Chicago: Open Court.

———, and Seung-Chong Lee. 1994. *Derrida and Wittgenstein.* Philadelphia: Temple University Press.

Geertz, Clifford. 1973. *The Interpretation of Cultures: Selected Essays.* New York: Basic Books.

———. 1983. *Local Knowledge: Further Essays in Interpretive Anthropology.* New York: Basic Books.

Geras, Norman. 1995. *Solidarity in the Conversation of Humankind: The Ungroundable Liberalism of Richard Rorty.* London: Verso.

Gitlin, Todd. 1995. *The Twilight of Common Dreams: Why America Is Wracked by Culture Wars.* New York: Henry Holt.

Goody, Jack. 1977. *The Domestication of the Savage Mind.* Cambridgeshire: Cambridge University Press.

Haack, Susan. 1993. *Evidence and Inquiry: Towards Reconstruction in Epistemology.* Cambridge, MA: Blackwell.

Hartnack, Justus. 1965. *Wittgenstein and Modern Philosophy.* Translated by Maurice Cranston. Notre Dame, IN: University of Notre Dame Press.

Havelock, Eric A. 1963. *Preface to Plato.* Cambridge, MA: Belknap.

Hegel, Georg Wilhelm Friedrich. 1956. *Lectures on the Philosophy of History.* Translated by J. Sibree. New York: Dover.

Heidegger, Martin. 1962. *Being and Time.* Translated by John Macquarrie and Edward Robinson. New York: Harper & Row.

———. 1971. *Poetry, Language, Thought.* Translated by Albert Hofstadter. New York: Harper & Row.

———. 1972. *On Time and Being.* Translated by Joan Starnbaugh. New York: Harper & Row.

———. 1977a. *Basic Writings from "Being and Time" (1927) to the "Task of Thinking" (1964).* Edited by David Farrell Krell. New York: Harper & Row.

———. 1977b. *The Question Concerning Technology and Other Essays.* New York: Harper & Row.

———. 1993. *Basic Writings.* Edited by David Farrell Krell. San Francisco: HarperCollins.

Hollinger, David A. 1995. *Postethnic America: Beyond Multiculturalism.* New York: Basic Books.

Hughes, Robert. 1991. *The Shock of the New.* Rev. ed. New York: Knopf.

Hume, David. 1958. *A Treatise of Human Nature.* Rpt. ed. 3 vols. Edited by L. A. Selby-Bigge. Oxford: Clarendon.

———. 1962. *Enquiries Concerning Human Understanding and [An Enquiry] Concerning the Principles of Morals.* Edited by L. A. Selby-Bigge. Oxford: Clarendon.

James, William. 1978. *Pragmatism, a New Name for Some Old Ways of Thinking; The Meaning of Truth, A Sequel to Pragmatism.* Cambridge, MA: Harvard University Press.

Jameson, Fredric. 1991. *Postmodernism, or, The Cultural Logic of Late Capitalism.* Durham, NC: Duke University Press.

Jones, W. T. 1969. *A History of Western Philosophy.* 2nd ed. New York: Harcourt, Brace.

Kant, Immanuel. 1929. *Immanuel Kant's Critique of Pure Reason.* Translated by Norman Kemp Smith. London: Macmillan.

———. 1956. *The Critique of Practical Reason.* Translated by Lewis White Beck. Indianapolis, IN: Bobbs-Merrill.

———. 1986. *The Critique of Judgement.* Translated by James Creed Meredith. Oxford: Clarendon Press.

———. 1987a. *The Critique of Judgement.* Translated by Werner S. Pluhar. Indianapolis, IN: Hackett.

———. 1987b. *The Fundamental Principles of the Metaphysic of Morals.* Translated by T. K. Abbott. Buffalo, NY: Prometheus.

Kemp, John. 1968. *The Philosophy of Kant.* New York: Oxford University Press.

Kenney, Anthony, ed. 1994. *The Wittgenstein Reader.* Cambridge, MA: Blackwell.

Kosinski, Jerzy. 1970. *Being There.* New York: Bantam.

———. 1978. *The Painted Bird.* Rev. ed. New York: Bantam.

Kripke, Saul A. 1982. *Wittgenstein on Rules and Private Language: An Elementary Exposition.* Cambridge, MA: Harvard University Press.

Kruger, Barbara. 1990. *Love for Sale: The Words and Pictures of Barbara Kruger.* Text by Kate Linker. New York: H. N. Abrams.

Kundera, Milan. 1984. *The Unbearable Lightness of Being.* Translated by Michael Henry Heim. New York: Harper & Row.

———. 1986. *The Art of the Novel.* Translated by Linda Asher. New York: Harper & Row.

Levine, George, ed. 1993. *Realism and Representation: Essays on the Problem of Realism in Relation to Science, Literature, and Culture.* Madison: University of Wisconsin Press.

Lévi-Strauss, Claude. 1961. *Tristes Tropiques.* Translated by John Russell. New York: Atheneum.

Locke, John. 1959. *An Essay Concerning Human Understanding.* Collated and annotated by Alexander Campbell Fraser. New York: Dover.

Lyotard, Jean-François. 1984. *The Postmodern Condition: A Report on Knowledge.* Translated by Geoff Bennington and Brian Massumi. Minneapolis: University of Minnesota Press.

———. 1988. *The Inhuman: Reflections on Time.* Translated by Geoffrey Bennington and Rachel Bowlby. Stanford, CA: Stanford University Press.

———. 1992. *The Postmodern Explained: Correspondence 1982–1985.* Translated by Don Barry et al. Translation edited by Julian Pefanis and Morgan Thomas. Minneapolis: University of Minnesota Press.

Malachowski, Alan R., ed. 1990. *Reading Rorty: Critical Responses to "Philosophy and the Mirror of Nature" (and Beyond).* Oxford: Blackwell.

Manuel, Frank E. 1968. *A Portrait of Isaac Newton.* Washington, DC: New Republic Books.

Marx, Karl. 1954. *The Communist Manifesto.* Translated by Samuel Moore. Chicago: H. Regnery.

———. 1956. *Selected Writings in Sociology & Social Philosophy.* Translated by T. B. Bottomore. Edited by T. B. Bottomore and Maximilien Rubel. New York: McGraw-Hill.

———, and Friedrich Engels. 1964. *The German Ideology.* Translated by S. Ryazanskaya. Moscow: Progress Publishers.

Maysles, David, Charlotte Zwerin, and Albert Maysles. 1978. *Running Fence.* Videorecording. 58 min. New York: Maysles Films.

Minor, Vernon Hyde. 1994. *Art History's History.* Englewood Cliffs, NJ: Prentice-Hall.

Mitchell, W.J.T. 1985. *Against Theory: Literary Studies and the New Pragmatism.* Chicago: University of Chicago Press.

Montaigne, Michel Eyquem, Seigneur de. 1958. *The Complete Works of Montaigne: Essays, Travel Journal, Letters.* Translated by Donald M. Frame. Stanford, CA: Stanford University Press.

Moravia, Sergio. 1995. *The Enigma of the Mind: The Mind-Body Problem in Contemporary Thought.* New York: Cambridge University Press.

Nietzsche, Friedrich. 1956. *The Birth of Tragedy; and, Genealogy of Morals.* Translated by Francis Golffing. New York: Anchor.

———. 1968. *Twilight of the Idols; and, The Anti-Christ.* Translated by R. J. Hollingdale. Harmondsworth: Penguin.

———. 1973. *Beyond Good and Evil; Prelude to a Philosophy of the Future.* Translated by R. J. Hollingdale. Harmondsworth: Penguin.

Noyes, Russell, ed. 1956. *English Romantic Poetry and Prose.* New York: Oxford University Press.

Nussbaum, Martha. 1994. "Feminists and Philosophy." *New York Review of Books* 11.17 (October): 59–63.

Olson, David R. 1994. *The World on Paper: The Conceptual and Cognitive Implications of Writing and Reading.* New York: Cambridge University Press.

Ong, Walter J. 1982. *Orality and Literacy: The Technologizing of the Word.* New York: Methuen.

Plato. 1968. *The Republic of Plato.* Translated by Allan Bloom. New York: Basic Books.

Poster, Mark. 1990. *The Mode of Information: Poststructuralism and Social Context.* Cambridge, MA: Polity.

Putnam, Hilary. 1995. *Pragmatism: An Open Question.* Cambridge, MA: Blackwell.

Rachels, James. 1986. *The Elements of Moral Philosophy.* New York: Random House.

Racine, Jean. 1991. *Phèdre.* Videorecording. 93 min. Sandy Hook, CT: Video Images.

Rice, Philip, and Patricia Waugh, eds. 1989. *Modern Literary Theory: A Reader.* London: Edward Arnold.

Rorty, Richard. 1980. *Philosophy and the Mirror of Nature.* Manchester: Manchester University Press.

———. 1982. *Consequences of Pragmatism: Essays, 1972–1980.* Minneapolis: University of Minnesota Press.

———. 1989. *Contingency, Irony, and Solidarity.* New York: Cambridge University Press.

———. 1990. "Feminism and Pragmatism." *Michigan Quarterly Review* (Spring): 231–58.

———. 1991a. *Objectivity, Relativism, and Truth: Philosophical Papers, Volume 1.* New York: Cambridge University Press.

———. 1991b. *Essays on Heidegger and Others: Philosophical Papers, Volume 2.* New York: Cambridge University Press.

———. 1992. "The Intellectuals at the End of Socialism." Presentation at California State University, Northridge.

———. 1993a. "Human Rights, Rationality, and Sentimentality." *Yale Review* 81.4 (October): 1–20.

————. 1993b. "Putnam and the Relativist Menace." *Journal of Philosophy* 90 (September): 443, 461.

————. 1994. "Does Academic Freedom Have Philosophical Presuppositions?" *Academe* 80.6 (December): 52–63.

————. 1995. "Movements and Campaigns." *Dissent* (Winter): 55–60.

Rousseau, Jean-Jacques. 1913. *The Social Contract and Discourses.* Translated by G.D.H. Cole. London: Dent.

Russell, Bertrand. 1959. *The Problems of Philosophy.* Oxford: Oxford University Press.

Saatkamp, Herman J., Jr., (ed.). 1995. *Rorty and Pragmatism: The Philosopher Responds to His Critics.* Nashville: Vanderbilt University Press.

Sacks, Oliver. 1990. *Seeing Voices: A Journey into the World of the Deaf.* New York: HarperCollins.

Salinger, J. D. 1981. *The Catcher in the Rye.* New York: Bantam.

Sartre, Jean-Paul. 1956. *Being and Nothingness: An Essay in Phenomenological Ontology.* Translated by Hazel E. Barnes. New York: Philosophical Library.

————. 1963. *Saint Genet: Actor and Martyr.* Translated by Bernard Frechtman. New York: G. Braziller.

————. 1965. *Anti-Semite and Jew.* Translated by George J. Becker. New York: Schocken.

Saussure, Ferdinand de. 1974. *Course on General Linguistics.* Translated by W. Baskin. London: Fontana/Collins.

————. 1983. *Course in General Linguistics.* Edited by Charles Bally and Albert Sechehaye. Translated by Roy Harris. London: Duckworth.

Shakespeare, William. 1958. *Hamlet.* New York: Washington Square.

————. 1961. *The Tempest.* New York: Washington Square.

————. 1968. *A Midsummer Night's Dream.* New York: Washington Square.

Shklar, Judith N. 1984. *Ordinary Vices.* Cambridge, MA: Belknap.

Shweder, Richard A. 1991. *Thinking through Cultures.* Cambridge, MA: Harvard University Press.

Sim, Stuart. 1992. *Beyond Aesthetics: Confrontations with Poststructuralism and Postmodernism.* Toronto: University of Toronto Press.

Sowell, Thomas. 1994. *Race and Economics.* New York: Basic Books.

Stendhal [Marie Henri Beyle]. 1953. *The Red and the Black; A Chronicle of the Nineteenth Century.* Translated by C. K. Scott Moncrieff. New York: Modern Library.

————. 1961. *The Red and the Black; A Story of Provincial France.* Translated by Charles Tergie. New York: Collier.

Stroud, Barry. 1977. *Hume.* London: Routledge and Kegan Paul.

Szasz, Thomas S. 1970. *The Manufacture of Madness: A Comparative Study of the Inquisition and the Mental Health Movement.* New York: Dell.

Taylor, Charles. 1994. "The Politics of Recognition." In *Multiculturalism: Examining the Politics of Recognition*, edited by Amy Gutmann, 25–73. Princeton, NJ: Princeton University Press.

Taylor, Richard, ed. 1974. *The Empiricists.* Garden City, NY: Anchor.

Todorov, Tzvetan. 1983. *The Conquest of America: The Question of the Other.* Translated by Richard Howard. New York: Harper & Row.

Voltaire [François Marie Arouet]. 1959. *Candide.* Translated by Lowell Blair. Toronto: Bantam.

———. 1980. *Letters on England.* Translated by Leonard Tancock. New York: Penguin.

Vonnegut, Kurt, Jr. 1973. *Breakfast of Champions; or, Goodbye Blue Monday.* New York: Dell.

———. 1989. *Wampeters, Foma, and Granfalloons.* New York: Dell.

Walker, Alice. 1973. "The Diary of an African Nun." In *In Love & Trouble: Stories of Black Women,* 113–19. New York: Harcourt, Brace, Jovanovich.

Weber, Max. 1958. *The Protestant Ethic and the Spirit of Capitalism.* Translated by Talcott Parsons. New York: Scribner.

Wheale, Nigel, ed. 1995. *The Postmodern Arts: An Introductory Reader.* New York: Routledge.

Wideman, John Edgar. 1994. *Fatheralong: A Meditation on Fathers and Sons, Race and Society.* New York: Pantheon.

Wittgenstein, Ludwig. 1947. *Tractatus Logico-Philosophicus.* New York: Harcourt, Brace.

———. 1958. *Philosophical Investigations.* Translated by G.E.M. Anscombe. New York: Macmillan.

———. 1969. *The Blue and Brown Books.* Edited by Rush Rhees. Oxford: Oxford University Press.

———. 1974. *Philosophical Grammar.* Edited by Rush Rhees. Translated by Anthony Kenny. Oxford: Blackwell.

Woolf, Virginia. 1927. *To the Lighthouse.* New York: Harcourt, Brace.

Wordsworth, William. 1967. *Wordsworth: Poetry and Prose.* Edited by W. M. Merchant. Cambridge, MA: Harvard University Press.

Workman, Chuck, dir. 1990. *Superstar: The Life and Times of Andy Warhol.* Videorecording. 91 min. Van Nuys, CA: Marilyn Lewis Entertainment Ltd.

Wright, Richard. 1965. *Uncle Tom's Children.* New York: Harper & Row.

———. 1966. *Black Boy: A Record of Childhood and Youth.* New York: Harper & Row.

X, Malcolm. 1964. *The Autobiography of Malcolm X.* New York: Ballantine.

———. 1991. *Malcolm X: Speeches at Harvard.* Edited by Archie Epps. New York: Paragon House.

Zimmerman, Michael E. 1990. *Heidegger's Confrontation with Modernity: Technology, Politics, Art.* Bloomington: Indiana University Press.

Index

Author

Ray Linn is a high school teacher in Los Angeles. For several years he was an English teacher at Jordan High School in Watts, and for the past few years he has been a philosophy teacher at Cleveland Humanities High School, an integration magnet in Reseda. He has also done consulting work with the Los Angeles Educational Partnership, both the Panasonic and Rockefeller Foundations, and the Modern Language Association. For his postmodern ideas about motivation, see "Fight Training in the High School Classroom" in *Advocacy in the Classroom*.